STOP THE MADNESS!

S • P • S
Publications

STOP THE MADNESS!
A Quick and Effective Guide to
Interrupting Irresponsible Behavior in Any Setting:
*Home • School • The Workplace • Corrections •
Treatment and Counseling Centers*
With Appendices that include quick-reference materials and
The Non-Dictionary of Another Usage

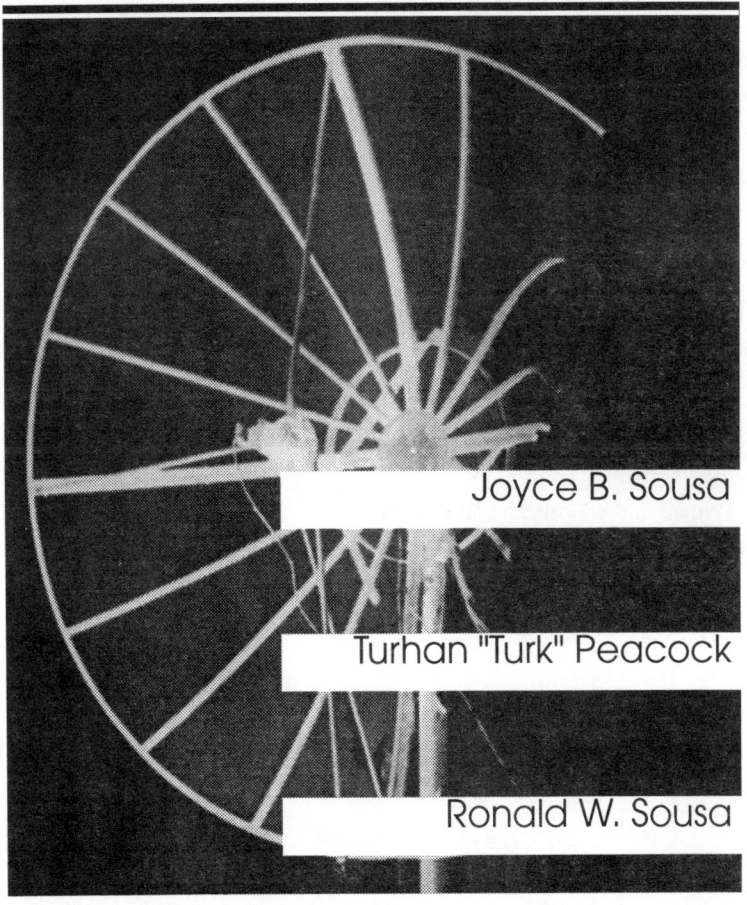

Joyce B. Sousa

Turhan "Turk" Peacock

Ronald W. Sousa

Copyright © 1998 by Sousa, Peacock, Sousa & Associates, Inc.

Second Printing, 2000.

All rights reserved. No part of this publication may be reproduced, stored in a retrieval system, or transmitted, in any form or by any means, electronic, mechanical, photocopying, recording, or otherwise, without the prior written permission of the publisher.

SPS Publications are published by Sousa, Peacock, Sousa & Associates, Inc.

328 N. Neil Street

Champaign, IL 61820.

Printed in the United States of America.

Cover design and book layout by Jonathan D. Sousa

Cover photograph © 1998 by Jonathan D. Sousa

ISBN 0-9665078-0-0

Dedication

This book is dedicated to all those individuals who in their private lives and/or professional capacities are struggling to create opportunities for change in the lives of our society's most challenging sons and daughters. Our special acknowledgment to those we have worked with along the way who have encouraged us by coming back to say that this *does* work.

Contents

Preface 1

1: "Madness" Defined 15

2: Working with the
           Irresponsible Thinker 43

3: How to Begin:
           Sanctions and Consequences 61

4: The Interruption Process 79

5: Know Your Own Thinking
           Errors and Vulnerabilities 115

6: What to Expect 129

Afterword:
   Extensions and Applications 137

Appendices:
   Materials 145

   The Non-Dictionary of
           Another Usage 153

Preface

We would like to start this book by making a couple of very obvious points. The first is that current treatment methods seeking to deal with the child or adolescent who acts out, the unreliable employee, the repeat offender, and other similarly problematic people have not been effective in bringing about significant change. Second, if you are a parent, counselor, teacher, or employer of such individuals you have almost surely witnessed their irresponsible behavior grow progressively worse.

If this is your experience and you have found yourself at your wits' end, the methods and principles we intend to set out in the following chapters will, we believe, have several healthy effects. Even if they do not promote basic change in such individuals, they will certainly prove effective in interrupting their irresponsible behavior, thereby enabling you to carry on your classroom, business, home life, etc. in a more orderly manner and also alleviating the amount of frustration, burnout, and helplessness you experience in dealing with bothersome and disruptive behavior.

We do not make this claim idly: the three of us, coming from diverse personal and professional backgrounds have separately realized the incredible effectiveness of the methods and principles about to be presented.

We shall each in turn talk a bit about our experience.

Joyce

I came upon the concepts underlying much of what we have developed and systematized in this book long before I realized their value. I had spent many years as a professional feeling useless and frustrated in my work with persistently irresponsible individuals, many of whom had been arrested. From the earliest moments of my work as an intern while pursuing my Masters at the Alfred Adler Institute in Minnesota, I felt that something was not right in my counseling interactions with the individuals I was attempting to help. While I never doubted their desire for change, not only did I seldom see such change occur, but I felt my efforts to help fell far short of the mark. When my husband took a new position at the University of Illinois and we left Minnesota, I made a personal commitment that if I resumed working with individuals having persistent difficulties in their lives due to irresponsible behavior, I would have to find a way to work with them that was more effective than what I had been doing.

What began as a search for a more effective form of treatment for residents in the Champaign County Correctional Center grew into understanding of a theoretical model and a method for structuring interactions with irresponsible individuals. Their effective use was potentially great, spanning the range of settings in which irresponsible behavior is found: homes, schools, businesses, counseling and treatment centers, as well as corrections. What soon became clear as Turk, initially my sole business partner, and I began developing and sharing this approach was that what we present in this book has a broad application and makes immediate sense to people in their personal and professional lives. We would speak to an audience about criminals and have parents come up and say "That sounds just like our son/daughter. Will you teach us how to use this material as parents?" Or business people would stop us after a similar presentation and ask if we could give them some information about how to relate our subject matter to a business setting. As is often the case, the more we spoke about what we were doing the more we ourselves learned about its value and its implications. The approach we were using and sharing was much more than a counseling technique; it was also an effective way to interact with the irresponsible people in our lives whatever our relationship with them might be. It was in addition a way to emerge from such an interaction without feeling exhausted or beset by a sense of futility. And a hidden benefit was that the more we used the material the more we were able to make better choices in our own lives as well.

Now not only was I being effective in assisting persistently irresponsible individuals in a change process they desperately wanted, but something much larger was unfolding before Turk and me. The approach we presented seemed to fulfill a need in the people we met. The information seemed to help them to understand better some of the troubling aspects of both their personal and their professional lives and to show them a way to help bring about changes. Increasingly we were told by teachers with whom we worked: "I am using this at home with my kids, and our home life is really improving." Or, parents with whom we worked would ask "When are you guys going to get this introduced into the schools?" Individuals active in their churches would ask if we would come to speak to their congregations or their youth groups. So we decided to write this simple book with the goal of sharing as effectively as we can with a wider audience one aspect of what we do. It is my hope that those who read the book will find in it possibilities not only for addressing personal problems in a more helpful and respectful way but, should such be appropriate, for functioning better professionally. It is also my hope that readers will see the broader implications for our communities: more effectively-designed intervention programs and a better understanding between institutions and individuals working in such programs both about the nature of the problem and about an effective way to address it.

I cannot imagine having come so far down this road without Turk, my friend and partner. The doors the two of us have knocked on, the ears we have bent, and the heartaches and laughter we have shared in this endeavor are rare and special indeed. In fact, we have worked on this material together for so long now that we are told that when one of us stops for breath in a presentation the other finishes their sentence. This introduction of mine should, then, not end without my mentioning this very special relationship.

Turk

My convictions about the effectiveness of the approach with which we have been working were born first out of personal experience. I began as a child who enjoyed the excitement of getting away with the forbidden. I learned early how to lie and manipulate in order to avoid being held accountable. I was the child who stole money off of my parents' dresser, who went places that I knew I wasn't supposed to go and hung around the guys my parents had told me not to hang around. As I look back, I see this behavior becoming a pattern in my life when I was six or seven years old. This is when I began stealing from my friends' parents, from my teachers, and later candy from stores. I was able to continue this pattern even when I got caught because the caring adults in my life believed that this must be some phase I was going through. Instead of being held accountable and having to face consequences for my choices, I would sometimes be given breaks. I would be told things like: "you're too smart to be doing things like this," "you know better," "you're such a nice person, you don't have to act like that." All of this may have been true and if I had been a basically responsible child I probably would have responded to a gentle nudge in the right direction. However, I was not a basically responsible child. Instead, my consistent choice to break rules, lie, manipulate and disregard advice and instructions as a pattern in my early life culminated in later years in my being repeatedly arrested and convicted of crimes in conjunction with many years of cocaine/crack abuse.

I was first introduced to methods like those about to be presented here in a substance abuse treatment facility in Indianapolis, Indiana in 1988. Upon entrance into this program the first concept that became immediately apparent to me was that I would not be allowed to blame my condition on anything other than the irresponsible choices I had been making in my life. The second critical concept I learned was that not only would no one in the program accept excuses for any irresponsible choices, decisions, and behaviors but that immediate consequences would be given if I even attempted to offer an excuse.

I was able to change life-long patterns of irresponsible and criminal behavior by accepting responsibility and being willing to be held accountable. I was able to learn this by the people around me being willing to hold me accountable through consequences (no matter how uncomfortable it was for them to do so) and never to accept any excuses. Since that time, in my capacity as a counselor, facilitator, and trainer, I have witnessed in many different settings (home, schools, counseling centers and treatment facilities) the effectiveness of these methods not only in helping persistently irresponsible individuals change their destructive patterns but also in sharply diminishing the frustration and burn-out felt by the responsible people who deal with them.

Ron

In many respects I am a last-minute walk-on in this book project—indeed, in the entire professional endeavor upon which the three of us have embarked. Unlike Joyce and Turk, I am not a clinician (though as a result of our partnership I have begun to do some work in that area and to carry out research on problems emerging from treatment procedures). I am, rather, a lifelong researcher/educator. To be sure, I have long shared in Joyce's career goals and frustrations, as she has in mine. And we have each intermittently done reading in the other's field so we could work ideas through with each other. But when Joyce began to work in Adlerian psychology and then started to read in the area of cognitive psychology and cognitive restructuring, a true overlap in our intellectual/professional interests emerged, for I have long worked with issues of cognitive difference and psychological theory. The specifics of that overlap aren't important here. Suffice it to say that, for me, the connection has led to my reading of research that before I had seen in terms of theory now in an entirely new light: as a framework to be applied to work with problems close to home—with people we all interact with day in and day out and, by extension, with some large-scale societal problems. It has been a very exciting development for me, since I have always wanted theory and practice to come together but in this area I have never before seen the way to effect that melding.

At the same time that I was seeing old, theoretical material being transformed into new, practical stuff, I found myself interacting with Joyce and Turk on a practical basis of another sort: our dining-room table had become the site for their drafting of public presentations and grant proposals and for their planning of professional directions. And I found myself drawn into the process, first as interlocutor and impromptu ghost-collaborator in grant writing and gradually as someone with a voice on especially the educational dimensions of the concepts and materials they were developing and the work they were doing. At some point, it seemed appropriate to us all that I undergo some training and come more fully aboard the enterprise.

At this point, when we do trainings or are hired as consultants, since I don't do groups multiple times every week as Joyce and Turk do, I end up talking primarily about the wider implications of the Corrective Thinking approach, or about its theory. Unless, of course, we go to educational institutions where questions of classroom management or teaching methodology are involved—in which case I get a bigger part... As you can see, I'm still growing into my role in this complex partnership.

I don't want it thought, however, that my appreciation for the approach we shall be presenting here is limited to the academic and the theoretical. Over the past few years I have come to rely heavily upon it in my roles as academic administrator and classroom teacher. It has provided me with a way to think about everything from the structuring of meetings involving professionals in conflict to the negotiation of awkward classroom situations and the handling of difficult students. And the methods it presents have given me a way to interact effectively in those situations. I'm certainly not going to make the claim that every situation was handled well or has ended positively, but a much greater number than ever before have in fact come out well. And since I had been doing all those same things for years before, it is abundantly clear that the approach presented here and the principles underlying it have made me more effective—and also enabled me to know where to invest my effort and where not. It has, then, become an invaluable part of how I do my various jobs.

When all is said and done, however, the main value that this entire experience has had for me is that of working with

Joyce and Turk to understand the effects of what we are doing and to develop more techniques and materials to try to maximize our impact and push ever further the questions we ask and the answers we come up with. The personal and professional camaraderie along the way has been wonderful—and I don't think that process is over yet. In fact, in some areas I think we've barely begun…

* * * * *

We three have joined together to try to present a method to interrupt patterned irresponsible behavior and the theory in which that method is grounded. In that endeavor, our different strengths seem to come together quite comfortably. We have chosen to write our preface this way in the hope that throughout the book you will hear and identify our individual voices as well as our collective one. We also hope you get as much out of reading the book as we have out of writing it.

Although our backgrounds are varied, we, along with the hundreds of parents, teachers, and counselors we have worked with and trained, have come to the same conclusion: **these methods work!**

Note

In the following pages, the concrete scenarios we present for illustration or example come from our clinical experience with individuals and groups. Specific details have sometimes been transposed from one case to another, and other specifics altered, in order to safeguard client confidentiality. The other examples of situations and language use more or less directly reproduce clinical experience as well.

1: "Madness" Defined

Scenario 1:

As Jimmy enters the classroom he tosses some trash in the direction of the waste basket and then meanders on to his seat. The wadded-up papers scatter on the floor. Mr. Pierson, the 9th-grade teacher, looks up from his desk, stands up, and walks over to the scattered trash.

Mr. Pierson: "Jim! Pick this up please."

Jimmy: "You gonna make me?"

Mr. Pierson: "You know the class rules. I'm asking you to pick up this trash you threw on the floor!"

Jimmy: "It's your rule; you do it! What's the big deal about paper on the floor anyhow? You some sort of fanatic?"

Mr. Pierson: "That's enough. You keep up that backtalk and you'll be asked to leave. I'm giving you one last chance to pick up the trash."

Jimmy: "F— you. You act like you own the place. I can never do anything right in your class. I'm leaving anyway."

Jimmy slams out the door.

* * * * *

This scenario will provide the reference for several of the main points we wish to make; we shall therefore return to it several times in the following pages. For now, let's merely pose some questions: Do any of the basic elements of this interaction sound familiar? Do they conjure up images of home, or of the workplace? If so, you should read on. Many of the elements in the above exchange are repeated in countless other scenarios. A few examples in brief:

- You are in a waiting room and a father with two children comes in. One of the kids spies a gum machine and asks for a quarter. The father says "no, I didn't bring any money with me." The child spits in her father's face and begins to hit him.
- A teacher begins a history lesson in class and makes the simple request that the students get out their books and homework. One student swears rudely and loudly at her and threatens her physical safety.
- An employee comes in late for the third time in the week. His supervisor approaches him and questions him about this pattern. The employee calls him a name and walks out swearing revenge.
- Two caring parents who want to do the best for their young daughter stand bewildered as she berates them and proceeds to do damage to the inside of their house. This is a reaction to a birthday gift that hasn't met her approval.
- An adolescent being questioned by his parents for cutting classes at school and staying out past curfew yells, screams, and curses in response and threatens them with physical violence.

Something is wrong here. This sounds crazy to a responsible person. Does any of it make sense? **This** is the madness—and, what is more, it is a very familiar madness in our contemporary society. Not only does something seem terribly wrong to us but we continually get a similar message of concern from a wide range of the people—from parents to social-service professionals—that we meet in talking about what has been called the "Corrective Thinking" model.[1]

Why this approach is effective

The principal reason why the approach is effective in helping both such irresponsible individuals as are described above to change their destructive patterns and also those responsible people involved in their lives is that it treats irresponsible behavior as a choice. Treatment of irresponsible behavior as a choice on the part of the person engaging in the behavior has several

---

[1] The term "Corrective Thinking," which we use generically to designate our orientation, was coined by David Koerner and Ronald Fawcett at the Beloit (Wisconsin) Project. We owe a considerable debt to Koerner and Fawcett, who were our trainers.

important values. It allows responsible people no longer to have to take responsibility for the actions of those individuals. As people who care about them, we no longer continually have to ask ourselves "What am **I** doing wrong?" when it is in fact not **our** behavior that is at issue. In addition, treatment of irresponsible behavior as a choice provides a key mechanism by which those who are behaving irresponsibly can be empowered to take responsibility for their own actions and therefore take control of their own lives.

Why do we follow the same child through school and watch an irresponsible pattern continue year after year? Why do we often then continue to deal with this same individual as an adult with irresponsible employment patterns? Why, indeed, do we often watch a sad but persistent march through life of a child who was troublesome as early as the first grade as he or she moves tragically on, eventually to take their place in the correctional system? Why are we still living with a recidivism rate that is unacceptably high? What is more, this child's life is usually littered with caring and concerned adults who have tried again and again to bring about a change. Lives of "difficult" children are often strewn with heartbroken adults who have struggled in vain and to exhaustion trying to interrupt this irresponsible pattern marked with tears, anger, frustration, and despair on all sides.

It is our experience that this failure to be as effective as we would like derives from the fact that most efforts focused on promoting change are designed by and for what we shall call basically "responsible" individuals—who, after all, are not the individuals we are hoping to change. By way of example of what we mean, let's look at some familiar refrains such as "Okay, I'll let it go this time," or "I'll give you a break this once, but don't let me see you do it again!" To a basically responsible thinker, to be on the receiving end of such gestures sets up a feeling of appreciation and obligation. A responsible individual will think about how grateful he or she is. A responsible individual will likely respond to such treatment with an effort not to repeat the irresponsible behavior. Such an individual will want to show that the "break" was not a misdirected gesture. A responsible person will not want the break- giver to be disappointed with the choice they made.

But let's take a look at someone we shall now call the "irresponsible thinker." This individual does not respond in the same way. A sense of obligation or of appreciation are missing. The irresponsible thinker will all but certainly interpret the break as "I got away with what I did." The sense of a debt owed, that key part of the dynamic that the responsible person in this example thinks they have set in motion, is absent. Any gratitude on the part of the irresponsible thinker is quickly gone, and old patterns are equally quickly resumed. Placing emphasis squarely on the irresponsible thinker's choice and then following out all of the implications that come from that focus make up the key first step in righting that imbalance.

The irresponsible thinker

What we are setting out to talk about here, then, is the vast and important difference between those we have up to now been casually designating as "irresponsible" and "responsible" thinkers. (We'll talk in a moment about how we dare use such sweeping terms.)

Consider the individual whose entire focus is on "me," on "obtaining what I want when I want it," on "having things my way." This individual is focused on getting what he or she wants and avoiding accountability. Such a thinking structure is not one that allows for appreciation and gratitude beyond that briefly given to someone who at a specific moment gives in to what the irresponsible individual wants. Moreover, any such gratitude is easily replaced by anger and revenge if the next demand is not dealt with in the same way. By and large this is a thinking structure that encourages relationships built on using and discarding. It is not one that permits change in the same manner that a responsible individual's thinking structure will allow for the correction of problem behavior. While specific behavioral features will vary from social group to social group, region to region, and individual to individual, people such as we describe here are to be found in every group and at every social level.

What we have come to understand is that to promote change we need first to recognize the thinking structure with which we are dealing and then develop a method for interrupting behavior and promoting change that is designed with that thinking structure in mind. This is not as difficult as it may sound. The "irresponsible thinker" we have been talking about has actually been studied, and we in fact know quite a bit about the general structures of his or her mental processes.

The basics of the Corrective Thinking approach are to be

found in the early work of Dr. Samuel Yochelson, his later collaboration with Dr. Stanton Samenow,[2] Samenow's own subsequent work,[3] and the systematic development of their lead into practical methods by David Koerner and Ronald Fawcett.[4] In brief, what all of those practitioners did, each following and building on the work of the former, was eventually to conclude that methods being used to treat irresponsible behavior were unsuccessful. In the main, that behavior remained resistant to traditional therapeutic methods of whatever sort. What these men chose to do as a result was to study the behavior patterns and thought processes of people who were behaving irresponsibly with an eye to developing a meaningful profile of such individuals and then developing techniques for intervening in those patterns and changing them. What they did, in essence, was to reject prevailing theory that dictates that you have to find causes and work from those causes in order to effect cures, saying instead that in this case such practice does not yield sufficiently

---

[2] Samuel Yochelson and Stanton E. Samenow, *The Criminal Personality*. 3 vols. New York, 1976-1986. (Vol. 1, 1976; vol. 2, 1985; vol. 3, 1986.)

[3] Stanton E. Samenow, *Inside the Criminal Mind*. New York, 1984; *Before It's Too Late*. New York, 1989.

[4] Dave Koerner and Ron Fawcett, Lifestyle Choices: A Curriculum for Responsible Living. Beloit, WI, 1994; Lifestyle Choices: A Curriculum for Responsible Living (Juvenile Version). Beloit, WI, 1994.

positive results. By contrast, the treatments developed using their approach, where systematically studied, have been shown to be extremely effective with varied clientele groups in a wide range of settings.

We shall spend the next few pages briefly going into the background of this approach. We have two principal reasons for taking this step. While our goal in this book is to introduce you to and familiarize you with a method for interrupting irresponsible behavior, we want you to understand something of the logic of the entire approach, so that you will be able to be as creative as possible within the method rather than merely carrying it out step by step in a mechanical manner and so that you will have a basic understanding of where it fits and what its uses (and limitations) are.

The purpose of this book is to present in detail a method for "interrupting" irresponsible behavior. By the term "interruption" we mean controlling an interaction with an irresponsible thinker so that it stays focussed on problem-solving. Such interruption can be an important part of a program to promote change in irresponsible thinkers—an important part, that is, of their basic reeducation. Indeed, such reeducation depends upon the consistent repetition and structuring of controlled interruption. In our Afterword we briefly discuss how such interactions are incorporated into a more thoroughgoing change process. For the present, we want to show you how to interrupt irresponsible behavior so that you can defuse negative situations, protect yourself from persistent frustration and burn-out, and take back control of your home, classroom, workplace, etc. If more profound change in the irresponsible individual is your goal, the material in this book will present some initial steps but may well not provide everything needed to reach that goal.

Let's get to the approach and its object, the irresponsible thinker. The following specific points used in the description of individuals with a pattern of irresponsible behavior come from the research and practical work of the practitioners mentioned above as well as from some of the basic principles of the psychology of Alfred Adler,[5] from corroboration we have received in the course of our work with parents, teachers, counselors, and corrections employees, and from our own experience in attempting to promote change with individuals ranging from young people having trouble in school and at home to repeat

---

5   See, e.g., *The Individual Psychology of Alfred Adler*, ed. Heinz L. Ansbacher and Rowena R. Ansbacher. New York, 1956. A useful digest is to be found in Rudolf R. Dreikurs, *Fundamentals of Adlerian Psychology*. Chicago, 1953.

criminal offenders. This description of the irresponsible thinker holds within it the tools we will use to construct an effective interruption process in the rest of this book. See if you don't recognize the irresponsible individuals in your lives in the following information.

The first thing we know about the persistently irresponsible individual is that much of what he or she does is done for excitement. It is important not to minimize this motive. The thrill of "getting away with it!" has a lot of appeal to this individual. If the opportunity for excitement doesn't present itself, the irresponsible individual will do something to generate that excitement: stir up trouble in some fashion, get into an argument with the teacher or an authority figure, skip school, steal a candy bar, etc. The prospect of life without this kind of excitement seems boring and pointless. For example, in the County Jail where we currently facilitate groups of offenders, it has been our experience that this reliance on excitement has acted as a serious roadblock to the change process. If there is nothing going on in the cell block, someone will generate some excitement—by initiating a power struggle over control of the television, the outcome of a card game, complaints about the general noise level, etc. We have seen persistent individuals go from one option to the another, until they are successful. And once the block is stirred up, additional trouble follows.

The second thing we know about this individual is their need for power and control. Slipping a candy bar into their pocket, or a shirt under their jacket in the store and walking out with it, while all those "other poor suckers" wait in line to pay is not only exciting but provides a tremendous sense of power and control. Just having a conversation with such an individual can quickly become a competitive battle. This is not accidental. The irresponsible individual, in their need for power and control, will seek to structure any interaction as a competitive one. "Your bed needs to be made," for example, will be answered by some version of "Make me." It is a daunting task just to communicate. Put-downs and challenges are roadblocks thrown up by the irresponsible thinker to avoid just that —communication. Statements will instantly be reframed as "putdowns" for example, or as demonstrations of disrespect ("You disrespecting me?"). This is an individual who quickly juggles to put everything on a win/lose basis—preferably "I win" and "you lose."

Scenario 2

Parents notice items showing up at home that they know their daughter would not have been able to buy. They suspect the items have been stolen from a friend's home, but they are not positive. When they try to engage their daughter in conversation about the subject, she quickly puts them on the defensive by challenging them to prove the items were stolen: "they were not." The parents respond: "they must have been." Etc.

* * * * *

Now here is the point that may be difficult to accept: it is effective to treat such behavior as the result of a choice. Note well what we say: "**to treat it as** the result of choice." To be sure, this individual may well not be equipped actually to choose among alternatives. He or she may be working with thinking patterns molded years before as the result of adaptions that were useful at the moment but not so for "responsible" development in the longer run. Yet it wasn't until we accepted the idea of dealing with irresponsible behavior as the result of a choice in the here and now and began working with these individuals on that basis that we began to see real effects. In our experience, work from that starting point is a vital part of any interaction whose goals are to be effective with the irresponsible thinker and to alleviate our own frustration. In the above scenario, the parents might have presented their daughter with the alternatives of 1) cooperating in gathering up the items, taking them back to the suspected theft site, inquiring if their absence had caused hardship, and compensating for any such hardship and/or facing any criminal consequences, or 2) continuing not to cooperate, in which case the entire matter would be turned over to the police.

This becomes confusing at times for those of us who care about, and are involved with, these irresponsible thinkers, whether they are our children, our students, our employees, or our clients. We tend to want to treat them as victims. Indeed, many of them have been victimized, some in terrible ways, and that victimization may have played a role in the fashioning of their maladaptive behavior. But many irresponsible thinkers have not been victimized. Moreover, the fact of victimization should not be seen as making it okay for any individual to harm another, commit a crime, disrupt a classroom and learning process for others, or make home a place of misery for other family members. The fact of victimization may make it more difficult for the individual to accept such principles and learn to choose socially-appropriate behavior, but it is not a reason for excusing or tolerating such behavior. The important point is that even though individuals who have led difficult and even tragic lives may have a more arduous version of the task in front of them, in the final analysis they have the same task that all people do: to learn to live responsibly.

It is also critical to remember that all victimized people do not become irresponsible human beings—in fact, only a small fraction do. And, conversely, people who seem to receive all of life's benefits do become irresponsible individuals. Thinking otherwise perpetuates the myth that irresponsible behavior and the troubles for us as a society that emanate from it are limited to the poor, to minorities, to the severely victimized, etc. We have not found this to be the case, nor do statistics bear out any such scenario. Troubled kids and adult criminals come from all sectors of society and all walks of life. We can treat the behavior of all of them as the result of a choice and build on that beginning.

And, speaking of "behavior," an important point that emerges from the work of the psychological researchers and practitioners cited above is to be clear that it is not the behavior itself that should be our focus but rather the thinking patterns, or lifestyle patterns, that enable specific behavior. While specific behaviors can signal to us certain underlying thinking patterns, we should not be convinced by simple change in behavior that basic lifestyle change has been effected, for shifts of irresponsibility from one area of activity to another are often quite easily made. (A child finally comes to behave responsibly at home and then starts to act out in school; an employee caught cheating on a time card moves to stealing pens and paper from the supply cabinet, etc.) Nor should simple change in behavior be the area of focus in the efforts that we make with these individuals. For instance, our methods in professional practice center around the replacement of clients' maladaptive thinking patterns with responsible ones in a reeducation program based in regular group meetings supported by individual homework (cognitive restructuring). Our goals do not involve dealing directly with behavior but rather addressing the thought structures that enable that behavior.

The final important point to be made regarding irresponsible individuals is to note that studies (e.g., Yochelson and Samenow) show that, despite wide differences in specific behaviors, there is much in common at the core of maladaptive thinking patterns. This is the most helpful information of all, for it gives us something relatively consistent with which to work. It is from understanding the irresponsible thinking framework itself that effectiveness in dealing with it comes to life.

The continuum of irresponsible behavior

Before we move on, we want to introduce the valuable concept of a continuum of irresponsible behavior.[6] (**Diagram 1**) We have come to rely on it in dealing with irresponsible thinkers. We mentioned above that we are going to focus on thinking rather than behavior, and it is in that regard that the continuum becomes really interesting. Consider the following.

---

[6] Again, the concept is owed to Yochelson and Samenow and to Koerner and Fawcett, and we have benefited from their various elaborations of it for our own rendition.

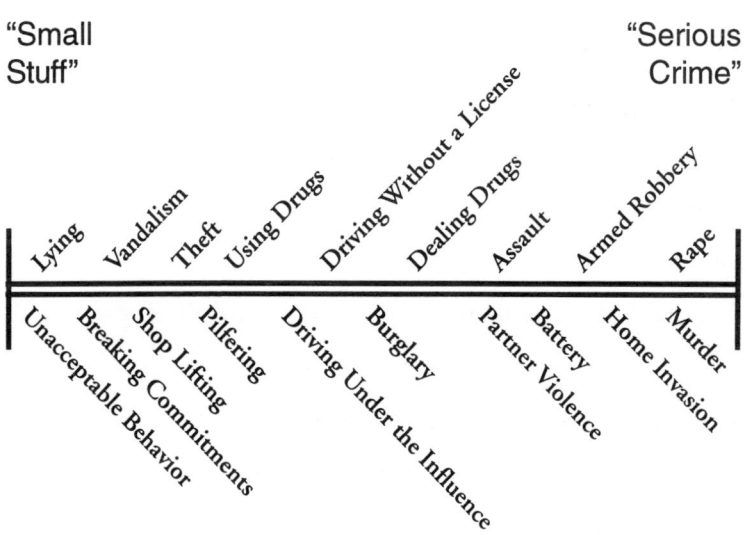

Diagram 1: Continuum of Irresponsible Behavior.

What does choosing to take money from your mom's purse have to do with choosing to chew gum in class knowing you will be sent to the principal's office have to do with choosing to steal a shirt from the store? What does choosing to stick up a gas station have to do with choosing to rape a woman have to do with choosing to take a life? This book and the interruption process that it espouses start from the premise that the commonality lies in "choice"—in the words "choose to." That is, it is our position that, for the purposes of effecting interruption and eventual change, the same thinking is taken to be involved in making it okay with yourself to take a small item as to take a valuable item. The same thinking process underlies an irresponsible act, no matter how seemingly small and insignificant or how enormous and cruel.

The importance of this concept for the interruption process is twofold. First of all, someone who, for example, has been active as an extreme criminal can be taught to think of such things as breaking promises and showing up late for work as dangerous because they allow him or her to engage in the same kind of thinking that was used in choosing to commit, say, an armed robbery. In other words, he or she can be made aware that they should not wait until they are again involved in serious crime to understand that they are in trouble. For an individual who wants to change lifestyle, this approach can be extremely helpful. It draws a connection between all of the irresponsible behaviors in their life. It allows that individual to see that slipping a candy bar in their pocket without paying is just as serious for them as sticking a gun in someone's face. The thinking that makes both of them all right is the same. To say that having what I want when I want it is more important than the rules, than the law, than another person's rights, or even than another person's life involves the same thinking process.

This is an area of frustration and confusion that constantly arises in our work with the parents of irresponsible adolescents. It often comes out in the group sessions that after their child had been doing so well, suddenly she or he relapses into irresponsible behavior. When we ask "What 'small stuff' have you been ignoring?", we more often than not get such answers as "they would come home a little later than we agreed," "they didn't always do their chores," "they would yell at their brother/sister." Parents in this situation face a great temptation to overlook "small stuff." When you are working with irresponsible thinkers, "small stuff" usually comes back to create bigger problems.

Secondly, for the youngster or adolescent who begins to show a pattern of irresponsible behavior at three, or five, or nine years old—which is a phenomenon that we observe in all (yes, all!) of the criminal offenders we work with—, the concept of a behavioral continuum based in common thinking patterns should alert all the adults who are concerned for this child to the importance of not dismissing or minimizing a developing pattern.

Notice that we deliberately use the word "pattern." A child who predominantly does their chores, homework, and what is asked of them and now and then makes an irresponsible choice is addressed differently from a child whose pattern it is not to get their homework done or the employee who persistently comes in late for work. (Hence our—admittedly overly general—terms "responsible thinker" and "irresponsible thinker." Clearly, the real picture is more complex than this, but it makes practical sense to think in terms of these two categories.) The individual who forgets as a pattern has a different thinking framework from the individual who forgets now and then. When an irresponsible pattern is seen, it is the pattern that needs to be addressed—with consistency and seriousness. Dismissing that pattern because the individual is young, male, likeable, etc., or because the behaviors are "minor" by current standards, is to show approval.

If you accept the premise that there are common general patterns to irresponsible thinking, then you understand why attention to behavior itself and the assigning of graduated seriousness to various irresponsible behaviors do not form part of our method. Rather, if you want to address irresponsible behavior effectively, you will pointedly address the thinking, not the specific behavior, and will do so with the same seriousness no matter what the behavior. This is not, then, to say that behavior is unimportant. But it is definitely to state that the interruption and change processes will take place not in an interaction based on behavior but in an interaction focused on the thinking process itself.

That thinking process for the irresponsible individual is one based predominantly on a small number of maladaptive thinking patterns. Let's take a brief look at those patterns.

Maladaptive thinking patterns[7]

The following is a list of the eight most common maladaptive thinking patterns (we alternately use the term "thinking errors" inherited from the studies we have cited). Take a moment to read through them.

---

[7] While this formulation is derived from our experience, we owe the concept of "maladaptive thinking patterns," or "thinking errors," to Koerner and Fawcett, who themselves synthesized from a much larger number of "thinking errors" described by Yochelson and Samenow.

Victimscript. Individual persistently blames others including family, friends, social conditions, etc:

> Language often indicative of this pattern:
> - "I couldn't help it. You know where I live."
> - "There's no getting along with that teacher."

Unrealistic self-image. Sees self as responsible despite actions:
- "Hey, I'm not a bad person. You act like this is a nuclear war."
- "Can anyone who can paint like this be all bad?"

Closed thinking. Unwilling to listen, to share information, or to be self-critical; goes on assumptions; lies, more likely by omission than by commission:
- "You're bogus. I suppose you think you know it all."
- "Why is this always about me?"

Sense of entitlement that extends to persons, places, and things; thoughts of intense jealousy:
- "Hey, she left it laying around didn't she? What did she expect me to do, leave it alone?"
- "He's got insurance."

Compartmentalized thinking. What happened before doesn't count, what happens now does not affect the future; what they want they want now. Little sense that behavior has consequences:
- "So what's your problem; I said I was sorry didn't I?"
- "I knew you'd bring that up; that was last year."
- "I won't get caught."

Inappropriate expectations about life that lead to boredom, an unwillingness to appreciate daily effort, and/or unreasonable fears:
- "I can't do it." (I.e., "I'm not willing to try.")
- "I can't get a job." (I.e., "I can't get the job I want.")
- "I can't believe this grade. It isn't fair. I stayed up all night for that test."

Control through power. Expects to be able to control situations and other individuals; uses manipulation and intimidation to achieve this goal; uses sex for power and control rather than for intimacy.

- "He made me hit him. He wouldn't do what I said."
- "I said 'now' and I meant it!"
- "I don't feel like it. Make me."

Specialness. A sense of being superior or unique; conviction that they are living in a "natural" state while "artificial" rules are for others:

- "Ten years to become a doctor? I can do it in four easy!"

* * * * *

Clearly, each of these broad patterns brings much within it, and the patterns are also intricately interrelated. Over the coming chapters you will gain considerable familiarity with the patterns and the specifics that they contain. Irresponsible thinkers regularly construct their lifestyle around some combination of the specific errors listed above. For now, the point is that many of these items should look familiar to parents dealing with problem children, employers dealing with difficult employees, and social-service professionals dealing with troublesome clients. Becoming familiar with the items in the list, perhaps even having them up on a wall to refer to, will be an important part of being effective in interrupting the irresponsible thinker(s) with whom you happen to be dealing. It is here that we are really hoping to change your focus as a parent, grandparent, teacher, counselor, or corrections officer. In whatever capacity you interact with irresponsible thinkers, you are going to focus on their thinking and not on their behavior. Doing this will change the nature of the interaction. We will talk more about this when we get to the interruption process in Chapter 4.

2: Working with the Irresponsible Thinker

Think about the following list.

An individual:
1. Tries to put others on the defensive, by:
   - attacking their competency
   - attacking them personally
   - attacking the competency of those in authority (staff, managers, parents, etc.)
   - claiming they don't appreciate any changes or efforts toward change that the individual may have made
   - bringing up irrelevant issues

- letting others do all the work (use of silence)
- minimizing the situation
- demonstrating anger
- picking at details
- paying little or no attention

2. Tries to control information, by:
   - agreeing with no intention of following through
   - saying whatever will please or satisfy at the moment (this includes saying "yes")
   - leaving information out, distorting information, mentioning self-serving information only
   - being intentionally vague
   - confusing others by including too much detail or not enough
   - refusing to give any information (silence)

3. Tries to control interactions, by:
   - listening selectively and hearing only what is self-serving
   - diverting attention to minor points

- insisting s/he "forgot" (in order to avoid being held accountable)
- focusing on being "misunderstood" as opposed to addressing the issue
- shifting to blaming others and/or circumstances[8]

* * * * *

These are what we shall be calling "tactics to avoid being held accountable and to maintain lifestyle." As with the "maladaptive thinking patterns" discussed in the previous chapter, their use by irresponsible individuals forms a pattern. The purpose of their use is, simply, to maintain the irresponsible lifestyle with which they have identified their very being. In effect, the individual wishes to protect their specific pattern of maladaptive thinking and, when confronting someone's attempt to hold them accountable for the negative results produced by that thinking, uses some set of these tactics to avoid that accountability. A

---

[8] These "tactics to avoid being held accountable and to maintain lifestyle" constitute our re-elaboration of Koerner and Fawcett's systematization of material originally developed by Yochelson and Samenow.

word of warning: most if not all people employ behaviors such as these in isolated circumstances—just as, for that matter, we all engage in some "maladaptive thinking patterns" now and again. We refer here only to a persistent pattern of their use to protect and maintain a lifestyle.

In our work with irresponsible thinkers, one of our primary goals is to interrupt irresponsible thinking and to instill responsible replacements. As we attempt to go about that task, one of our principal activities is the combating of tactics launched by the individuals involved. Those tactics have the single goal of preventing us—or anyone— from interfering with the developed lifestyles of these individuals.

What we have found most effective in reaching our goals begins with identifying the "tactics" beforehand (that is talking about them and what they represent) and then, in the particular situation, pointing out the specific tactic being used and stating our refusal to deal with it: "Sam, I'm going to stop you there. That is a tactic (or, that is the tactic of minimizing), and, as you know, we don't deal with tactics here." Needless to say, it is entirely likely, especially early in the interruption process with that individual, that this will merely produce the use of another tactic, with anger and hostility possibly coming to the fore as well. In upcoming chapters, we will show you how to react effectively in such situations and ultimately succeed in interrupting maladaptive thinking.

When one deals with irresponsible thinkers, the presence of tactics to avoid accountability and maintain lifestyle is not the only difficulty that will be encountered. There are others as well. Let's start out with differences in word meanings.

Scenario 3:

You had for several months been working in a counseling capacity with a youngish man. You had not seen that individual for a while, you pass him on the street, and he comes over to talk. In the conversation, you ask "How are things going?" "Oh, fine," he replies. You move on thinking how well that counseling had turned out. You imagine that family problems you discussed have improved, or that problems with peers have eased. Meanwhile, the man moves on down the street to meet some friends and spend the day doing drugs. He ends up participating in the robbery of a convenience store.

* * * * *

We suggest that this type of exchange in fact occurs very frequently when someone is trying to help another individual "get their life together," if that life has been one centered around a pattern of irresponsible behavior.

What happened in that encounter? Each person drew assumptions based on their own thinking patterns and common language meanings that arise within those patterns. The young man would be genuinely confused if you accused him of lying, but the counselor would very definitely feel that he or she had been deceived. What is "fine" in a responsible lifestyle is likely to be very different from what is "fine" in an irresponsible lifestyle. A responsible thinker says things are "fine" when daily tasks are being performed, bills are generally getting paid, responsibilities are being met, etc. An irresponsible thinker, by contrast, typically means something very different. He or she uses this phrase and similar ones to mean such things as "other people are staying out of 'my business'," "I am generally getting away with what I want to get away with," "I am, by and large, able to do what I want when I want it." Etc., etc., etc. And, most importantly, "I am not getting caught." Our two individuals simply passed one another, had a brief exchange, and thought they had communicated. If communication implies some level of mutual understanding, that is not at all what happened.

This is but a small example of many such confusing exchanges and miscommunications. In such exchanges, many common words like "friend," "respect," "justice," "fair," etc. will carry divergent meanings. The word "unfair," for example, is often used by individuals whose life is run on maladaptive thinking patterns simply to mean getting caught rather than getting away with something. These individuals regularly cry out "it isn't fair" when they are being held accountable. To work with such an individual and not to understand these differences is to be severely handicapped.[9] We know, because the three of us writing this book have functioned at various times with and without

---

[9] We have for several years engaged in a project of collecting examples of "irresponsible" language usage and include in our Appendices the version of our collection—which we have titled "The Non-Dictionary of Another Usage"—that is current at the time of this book publication. An important caution: please read the introductory material carefully before going into the list of terms, since there is potential for misuse of the collection.

this knowledge. The difference in effectiveness is startling. What before made little sense begins to be understood; more meaningful interaction emerges.

Irresponsible thinkers have long understood responsible principles. The world is primarily run on those principles, and they are pretty easy to spot. Irresponsible thinkers, having begun an irresponsible thinking pattern as children, therefore learn early in life about the "jerks" and "suckers" whom they choose to avoid. But by and large responsible people have understood irresponsible activity only as the absence of responsible activity. A full understanding of irresponsible thinking as a coherent system with its own patterns, meanings, and principles has largely been lacking.

The tendency, within the criminal justice system and in treatment programs of various sorts, has been to break this system up into bits and pieces: within the area of criminal activity, thieves are dealt with differently from murderers, from sex offenders, and so on. Youngsters who are consistently disrespectful in class are often dealt with as a separate problem from youngsters who are engaging in vandalism or physical violence. To miss the commonality of thinking underlying all of this behavior is to miss a chance to be effective. We are not saying that stealing some bills out of a wallet is as serious an activity as, for example, date rape, but what is key here is that there is a common thinking pattern in making it okay to ignore the rights of others. If we don't acknowledge that and address it, we miss a critical factor and allow ourselves as a society in general and as potential change agents in particular to minimize and pass on as harmless the youngster who is exhibiting an irresponsible pattern at an early age. We thus do that child and those who love him or her a great disservice. On the other end of things, if we give the message to someone recently released from prison that they are okay merely because they are holding down a job and aren't coming to the attention of the local police, we may well be setting them up to re-offend.

Scenario 4:

Mary has been in prison for theft, and her family, her parole officer, and her friends all have their eyes solely on the area of theft or similar criminality as indicator of her successful transition back into society. Meanwhile, she is not showing up regularly for work, driving without a license, and sometimes getting into verbal conflicts with her co-workers.

* * * * *

Indeed, Mary herself may well not know that she's in trouble. She too may be thinking that as long as she isn't committing theft everything is "fine." But it isn't. Sooner or later Mary is going to move down the continuum using that same irresponsible thinking pattern and do something socially categorizes as "more serious."

The question of drug use

A bit of information we want to mention concerns the use of drugs. It has been the case that **every** persistently irresponsible thinker with whom we have dealt who has also had substance abuse as a problem in their lives had a maladaptive thinking pattern before the drug use began. The use of chemicals certainly makes matters worse, accentuating the irresponsible pattern and perhaps accelerating the gravity of the behavior. But, in our experience, to lay blame for irresponsible behavior to the use of drugs is to miss the boat. To be sure, many of the people with whom we have worked plugged drug use into their lifestyle at some point—because it enhanced the excitement or lowered inhibitions. Ultimately, however, you can clean up an addict and sober up an alcoholic, but the irresponsible thinking pattern will still be there. Basic change will not have taken place.

The irresponsible thinking core

Now let's talk for a minute about something we have come to call "the irresponsible thinking core." (**Diagram 2** [p. 55]) Picture the sun as irresponsible thinking. Now picture the rays coming out from the sun as the various aspects of the irresponsible individual's life. These might be education, spirituality, work, relationships, and physical well-being, for example. If the irresponsible thinking core is not addressed, the relationships this individual has will tend to be abusive and perhaps violent. Employment records will show numerous job changes and dissatisfaction left behind. There will tend to be conflicts and quarrels on the job. This individual will usually make an unreliable employee. Not only will they often have an inconsistent attendance record but they may also be stealing from the job site. School history will be filled with problems. Reasons given will describe a pattern: the trouble, however it manifests itself, will have happened because of the teacher, the subject, the other kids in the class, and so on. Everything will be someone else's fault. Grades will never be fair. Poor performance will be because the "teacher had it in for me."

The point is that if we concentrate our efforts toward change on these various aspects of an individual's life without addressing the irresponsible thinking, we will be missing the mark. The conning, manipulating, lying, blaming, and unwillingness to take responsibility will all continue. If the thinking underlying these behaviors is not changed, the behaviors and attitudes will remain. The choices that the irresponsible thinker makes will continue to be the same. By that we mean that this individual will continue to choose to be deceitful, to blame others, not to learn from the past, to write off as "boring" anything that doesn't have the excitement of irresponsible activity, etc. This individual will continue to attack the person holding them responsible with name-calling, abuse, and threats, or any number of the tactics to avoid accountability.

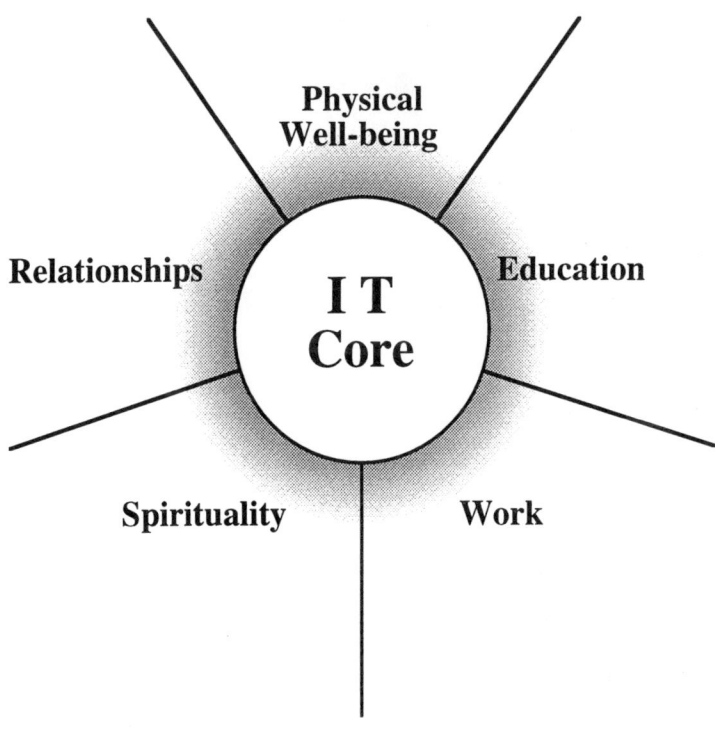

Diagram 2: The Irresponsible Thinking Core.

Closing the loop

This leads us to a concept we call "closing the loop" or "speaking the same language," which relates very directly to holding individuals accountable. What that concept refers to is the fact that often there are many people simultaneously working in one way or another with the irresponsible thinker. Take a child with a parent or guardian, a social worker, the school principal; perhaps a teacher is also involved, and let's add a probation officer. If all these adults are willing to hold this child accountable, this youngster will derive the benefit of receiving the same consistent message (as will, for example, the schoolchild and the employee mentioned above [p. 31] who shift their irresponsible behavior from one site to another). If, however, one or two of the players in this drama are "soft touches" and let the child off the hook for irresponsible, disruptive, or harmful behavior, then the chances of achieving what we are all working to accomplish—a change in thinking and behavior—has just been significantly lowered. Part of the structure of irresponsible behavior is an unwillingness to be held accountable. If the irresponsible thinker locates someone in the constellation of concerned people who is willing to "give them a break," guess who they are going to want to see? Correspondingly, guess who they will avoid at all costs? And if they can't avoid seeing or meeting the latter, they will certainly not want to listen to them. It is obvious how all this will work out. In our example, the adult who is letting this child continue to get away with their irresponsible thinking pattern will be told how "understanding" they are, while the adult consistently holding them accountable will be called "unfair" and "cold." Understanding what the irresponsible individual means when he or she uses such words and phrases is an important part of learning to persist, not to feel personally attacked, and ultimately to be effective in the interruption process.

* * * * *

The problem is, does the sort of approach we have been developing in these pages sound like the language we traditionally associate with care? It is difficult for us to believe that anyone who has dealt over time with irresponsible thinkers will not recognize the pattern we are pointing out. But a problem arises when we begin to discuss how to effect change. Holding an individual accountable to the point of frustrating him or her may not sound like the stance of someone trying to help. This is, however, precisely what this individual needs. Virtually every study ever done shows that the establishing of rules and boundaries is ultimately understood as an act of caring—though it will most surely not be received that way initially by someone already deep into an irresponsible lifestyle. Making exceptions, extending breaks, turning a blind eye, etc. only gives the irresponsible thinker a message of approval and simultaneously of lack of concern.

This might be the moment to put our efforts here in a proper perspective. We are not advocates of "spare the rod and spoil the child" or "lock-'em up and throw the key away" approaches to the problems we work with. Nor are we exponents of a moralistic approach to those problems. First and foremost, we advocate this approach because it is effective; nothing less—and nothing more. Moreover, we conceive of our approach as the ultimate expression of care—a care that is effective with people who are at risk. And, as you will see, as agents of intervention and/or change, we seek to interact with the irresponsible individual in a wholly respectful manner.

It is vitally important that we all take a good look at ourselves in this respect. (We will come back frequently to this crucial theme and in fact devote an entire chapter to it later on.) Change programs and systems created to address the problems of irresponsible behavior are often designed with societal comfort in mind rather than according to what best helps the individual change. It is not easy to hold someone who may be begging for help or insulting us to our face rigorously accountable. Yet this is precisely what we must do. If we cannot move beyond wanting to feel good, we will not be useful in the interruption and change processes. One of the goals of this book is to help those persons wishing to practice an effective interruption method understand that the most caring and empathetic thing we can do with and for people who have shown a pattern of irresponsible thinking and behavior is to show absolute consistency—and, at the same time, absolute respect—in holding them accountable for what they do.

All of this makes instant sense to those of us who interact with troubled kids and criminal offenders. Parents repeatedly express their extreme gratitude when we present this approach. Smiles of recognition spread over the faces of irresponsible adolescents. And repeat criminals grin and nod their heads at these concepts in acknowledgment of their validity. The consistency of such reaction is what keeps us motivated.

3: How to Begin: Sanctions and Consequences

We have spent some time now laying the background for the process we want to introduce. Remember that we have done so for several reasons, primary among them that we want you to understand the logic of the entire approach so that you can be creative, and therefore effective, in the interruption process we shall be presenting in Chapter 4. We are, however, all anxious to get to this section that talks about "How To Begin."

The first step has to do with sanctions and consequences. They play an important role in the interruption process. Irresponsible thinkers have developed an elaborate thought and behavior system designed to avoid consequences—or to deal with them as "unfair" when they become unavoidable. If irresponsible thinking and the behavior and attitudes that arise from it are to be successfully interrupted, consequences or sanctions need to be in place.

We use the terms more or less interchangeably in practice, but what we mean by each is as follows. A sanction is a rule that we make up saying, for example, that a certain behavior is unacceptable and, if it is engaged in, a negative consequence will be meted out to the person who engages in it. A consequence is the second part of the sanction, its "feedback" so to speak. Consequences are often already in place: the consequence of unwise actions are often unpleasant results (if X steals from the clothing store, she may go to jail). Sometimes, however, we shall have to establish "artificial" consequences (if Y doesn't do his chores, he will be grounded).[10] Sanctions and consequences should not be seen as punishment or as threats to make someone do what we want them to do. They should be seen as learning devices that will help in the development of responsible

---

[10] In understanding these distinctions we have benefited from the work of the Adlerian psychologist Rudolf Dreikurs, especially his *Children: The Challenge*. New York, 1964.

thinking patterns—as, in effect, representative of the restraints and consequences we all face and learn from in life.

Scenario 5:

The parents of a teenaged boy found out that their son had taken the car out on a joy ride. They told the son that he would be given a break this time but that if it happened again the police would be called. It happened again and the police weren't called. The subsequent time it happened, the police didn't have to be called: the child got into a wreck, and the family had to pay some $3,000.00 in repairs for the car and the other one in the accident. The boy went to court and was put on probation. Presumably because of the stringency of that consequence, the son has engaged in no further irresponsible behavior since the court date (whether or not his thinking patterns have been substantially changed is not yet known).

* * * * *

In this scenario "life" itself ended up providing the consequences that, for the good of all involved, should have been forthcoming from the parents. The sanctions and consequences were available and had been made clear. If the parents had followed through on them, they might have achieved the same effect sooner. Instead they in effect chose to demonstrate that the irresponsible thinking and behavior would not provoke the specified consequences, thus suggesting that both they and the thinking/behavior were not serious.

Whatever the setting in which you work, be it home, office, counseling agency, corrections, etc., the consequences that will result from making certain choices need to be spelled out clearly ahead of time. This is critical. There are a few important rules about sanctions and consequences that must be remembered to increase their effectiveness. In general, they should be appropriate to the nature and/or severity of the irresponsible behavior. Rule number two is that they need to be known up front. Third, consequences should get more serious as the thinking and behavior continue. Rule number four is that they should be able to be implemented as soon as possible—ideally within 24 hours. This is essential to learning, if learning (i.e., cognitive restructuring) is going to take place. And lastly, make certain that you are willing to enforce these sanctions fully and consistently. If enforcement is not carried out, more harm than good will be done. In addition, you will increase your own frustration and sense of futility, and the irresponsible person will merely be reinforced in their old thinking patterns. Not enforcing sanctions is a good way to perpetuate the dead-end cycle of threats, disappointing behavior, more threats, more broken rules, and on and on and on.

Let's take a look at some suggestions for sanctions and consequences that might be appropriate in different settings. Take the office first. Appropriate consequences, in order of increasing seriousness, might be: a discussion with a supervisor accompanied by a warning; a temporary demotion; a permanent demotion; firing. Once again, sanctions need to fit the logic of the environment in which they are being used. The specific sanctions aren't as important as the fact that they fit the general rules mentioned above and that they make sense in context.

How about in a counseling center? Counseling is often done within the restrictions of an agency environment, in which case individual counselors may not have a lot of freedom to create sanctions. A common policy for such irresponsible choices as not showing up might be to issue a bill for services unless 12 or 24 hours notification is given. Exceptions need to be clearly spelled out ahead of time. If groups are missed, the individual might be required to write an apology to the whole group. A certain number of absences would result in temporary or permanent removal from the group. These situations may require some imagination and effort. Those counselors in independent practice will have more leeway.

What about in the home? There are an endless number of consequences that can be used in the home environment, limited only by the logic of the specific situation and your creativity. Some parents we have worked with seem stumped by the idea at first but really take to the concept after they reach some comfort with its effectiveness and understanding of its usefulness in the interruption process. There is much more that can be done in addition to the popular consequence called "grounding." It is also important to fit the consequence to the child. Having as a consequence spending the afternoon in one's room for a child who is dying to do just that is—obviously—not going to be effective. Attention and effort need to be made to pick the appropriate consequences for the child and for the offense, and to have it make sense within the particular family structure. Keep sanctions and consequences as simple as possible. A system of sanctions that is overly complicated or detailed will be more difficult to carry out—and carrying it out is crucial. For parents we strongly recommend as a general principle the establishing of household chores—and of consequences for not getting them done. Consequences might be limiting phone use, curtailing contact with friends, or limiting time spent in favorite activities.

Effective parenting requires a commitment to be willing to do what needs to be done.

Scenario 6:

A father has grounded a teenaged daughter who has been acting out. Her favorite pastime is playing hockey at the end of the cul-de-sac. When the father is not home, she simply goes into the street and shoots goals into the net. The father, caught up in the heat of arguing with her, is unable to come up with a solution to this situation.

* * * * *

In this case, when the parent finally came to grips with the necessities of what he was facing, he found a strategy that worked: he simply made the portable hockey goal unavailable. (We all hope that the removal is but a short-term necessity!)

Occasionally the commitment to be willing to do what needs to be done may mean calling the police, or a probation officer (see again Scenario #2 [p. 28]). For a parent, doing this will not be easy, but understanding that it is the way respectfully and effectively to take back control of your own life, your family life, and hopefully to encourage the offending child to make more responsible choices, may require that you take that step.

This is a good moment to take an honest look at what our reluctance is about. We will discuss this more in Chapter 5, but let's spend a minute on that issue now. If, as we have already said, our goal as parents, or interrupters of irresponsible behavior, is to maintain our own comfort, we will often make harmful choices.

Scenario 7:

Parents are trying to get their teenaged son to go to our parent/adolescent group. The boy refuses until the parents finally agree to buy him the name-brand shoes he wants.

* * * * *

In effect, the boy holds the parents hostage until he gets the shoes he wants. Rather than having a system of sanctions and consequences in place to invoke for his choosing not to meet the expectation of attending group, the parents see the issue resolved by means of a power struggle. When that is the principal mode of conflict- resolution in such relationships, it is usually the party who becomes uncomfortable or frustrated first who loses. If, because of our own needs, we are unable to see our children disappointed or angry, our children will find great power in this vulnerability of ours. Effective parenting involves structuring proper choices for our children and then allowing them to experience the consequences of their choices. It requires that we have that courage. The only time we recommend interfering in this process is when someone's safety is involved.

The two-year-old who learns that the adult in charge will not enforce rules in public because of timidity or potential embarrassment has discovered a great source of power and one that he or she is not likely to give up voluntarily. The five-year-old who hits the mother who smiles nervously but takes no action has learned a lesson that may be irresponsibly employed as the child grows up. The youngster who makes eating dinner impossible for the family because of disruptive behavior and is sent away from the table but is given a snack later to appease his or her hunger is likely to draw some unfortunate conclusions from that result: "I can get away with disrupting dinner and get my dinner too." The child in Scenario #7 who gets the shoes he wants will draw structurally similar conclusions.

Sanctions and consequences are a critical piece of the learning process. It is by making choices and living with the consequences that each of us develops our own system of values. If we choose to stay up late watching a T.V. show and don't like the way we feel struggling through work the next day, we have learned some important information to be used in future choices. If we decide to go to a party instead of studying for an exam or finishing a paper that is due and don't do well in the course as a result, we have had the opportunity to experience how life usually works. This is a vital part of maturing. It is the way we all learn to choose one thing over another. If children are deprived of consequences, their choices may remain unwise and inconsistent, their expectations may be unrealistic and self-centered. It is the classic example of wanting their cake and eating it too: "out of my irresponsible thinking and lack of effort or interest in anything boring or disagreeable, I want the benefits that come with hard work and responsible choices."

What about sanctions and consequences in the school setting? This is certainly another challenging area for a number of reasons. A teacher works within a system that will first of all have its own set of district rules. Within them may be separate rules for each school, which are then further broken down into individual teacher and classroom rules. The latitude that each teacher has for setting sanctions and consequences may not be clear. In addition, what is allowed by one teacher may not be allowed by another. This is fertile ground for an irresponsible youngster to work. Such a situation takes us back to Chapter 2 and the importance of having everyone speak the same language. If a child can do something and know that one of the teachers will let them get away with it—again, guess what? The phenomenon of the youngster seeking out those not willing to hold them consistently accountable speaks to the degree of frustration many caring people feel when they work within a system in which everyone is doing something different. Such a fragmented system is an ideal environment for an individual whose goal is to avoid accountability. There is always some place to go where they can get what they want. It is thus not an environment that will support change as fully as we might like.

Ideally—and this is what we recommend when we work with educational settings—, there should be one clear set of sanctions and consequences for the institution. All staff would be aware of the hierarchy of consequences and be willing to enforce them. This would be the best of all worlds. Done, it works very well. We have worked with teachers who have initially been very discouraged by this task and felt it to be quite hopeless. That reaction is easy to understand since teachers often work within a system where individual classroom control is limited. Many teachers initially express the fear and concern that they will not be supported by administration. They also often feel vulnerable to attacks from unhappy parents. These are real and serious problems. Addressing them goes beyond the scope of this book. In settings where we do address these problems, we advise teachers, counseling staff, and administration to reach an agreement that will serve effectively to "close the loop." What is within the scope of this book is to give an idea of what is possible on an individual basis and within groups of teachers.

There is much that individual teachers can do to take control of their classrooms and receive the additional benefit of reducing their own frustration and "burn out." The groundwork can be laid by establishing some sanctions and consequences within the area over which you as a teacher have jurisdiction. These sanctions will, of course, be set up under the general rules that cover all sanctions: they are made clear ahead of time, they are graduated, they can be implemented within 24 hours, and you are willing and able to enforce them. If you have to undertake the introduction of Corrective Thinking on your own, we encourage you to go ahead and not feel discouraged. However, if you can do it as a group, you will get the benefit of additional support as well as the sharing of each others' experiences and ideas. Consistency in enforcing the sanctions, flexibility in adjusting your system if it is not working and in learning what you do **not** have to do will be your energy savers. There are schools in the United States where a version of this approach has been implemented—to excellent results.[11]

The other area that we want to mention briefly is corrections. It seems to us from our experience in working with corrections that adequate sanctions and consequences are already in place. The challenge is to see that they are applied within 24 hours and applied consistently. The same type of difficulty is present in corrections that teachers face, which is that if only some staff are being consistent while others give favors or look the other way, the system is flawed and relatively ineffective. All irresponsible thinkers will look for the weak link and use it to their advantage. One or two uncooperative staff members can sabotage an effective structure and make things difficult for their co-workers. Staff training is something we highly recommend as a way to attack this problem.

Some of you may be wondering why all the fuss about setting up sanctions and consequences and all the emphasis on consistency. We circle back to when we spoke, in Chapter 2, about troubles in communication. If two basically responsible

---

[11] For example, we have seen statistics for academic year 1993-1994 from Jackson Hole High School, Jackson Hole, WY indicating that installation of a Corrective Thinking approach to the school discipline program led to a decrease in student infractions of rules by at least 9% in all discipline categories and up to as high as 55% in the most affected category.

individuals are dealing with one another, the ground rules between them are usually understood. If I am an employer and call in an employee to discuss a problem, I assume certain things. If that employee is basically a responsible individual who is willing to be held accountable, I assume that he or she can be counted on to remain within certain boundaries: the discussion will stay on the problem at hand, there won't be any name-calling or verbal abuse, the employee will not throw anything, and I should not have to worry about my physical safety. These are assumptions that we cannot necessarily make when we confront an irresponsible thinker. Such uncertainty accounts for a good deal of the stress we undergo in working with them. Holding an irresponsible thinker accountable can be a very upsetting experience. You may be called several names. You may find it very difficult to stay on the topic you have chosen. You may find yourself engaged in self-defense—verbal and sometimes physical. You may be threatened. In other words, there is no common ground in the meeting of an irresponsible thinker and a responsible person over the former's irresponsibility. This common ground needs to be deliberately and overtly created. A critical part of having a successful interaction and reducing the stress is establishing this common ground ahead of time. This is where sanctions and consequences fit into the larger structure of the interruption process itself. Consider the following example.

If I am a parent confronting my child about the fact that the garbage has not been taken out, it is my job to make certain that the rules about this interaction are understood. If I am dealing with a basically responsible child, I do not have the same set of problems I do if I am confronting a child who persistently refuses to do what he or she is asked to do. In the latter case, I need to prepare in order to assure as well as I can that we are going to stay on the subject (that the garbage is not being taken out) and that I come out of the discussion not feeling frustrated and ineffective. We will lay out the fundamentals of setting up such an interaction in the next chapter. What we want to make clear in this chapter is that having a set of clear sanctions and consequences in place, whether it be at home, in the workplace, in your counseling office, or in a correctional setting, and having it known that they will be consistently enforced, is a critical part of constructing the kind of environment in which successful interruption can occur.

One final word. Enforcement of a system of sanctions and consequences with an entrenched irresponsible thinker will not only be difficult to accomplish, it will also be difficult to sustain, since the immediate results will likely be the heightening of tensions. Remember, this person is fighting to protect an entrenched lifestyle. It is important to remain committed to the process. In a significant percentage of cases, it will soon produce positive results.

Intervention/prevention

figures currently being bandied about suggest that, in the attempt to combat delinquency and criminality, strategies of intervention (i.e., those involving working with the individual after they have begun to engage in irresponsible behavior) are extremely costly while, by comparison, prevention is economical. The last ratio we heard was 25:1.

"Interruption," as we present it in this book, is definitely an intervention technique; we intend to show parents, teachers, social workers, employers, and others an effective tool for their use in dealing with the irresponsible thinker(s) in their lives. At the same time, it simultaneously functions as a prevention technique in several ways. First, the line after which an individual is committed to a lifestyle of delinquency or criminality is not a hard and fast one. If interruption is practiced early and consistently in situations where it is called for, it will act as a preventative to the continued development of such a lifestyle. Second, when the "loop is closed" through consistency at home and the public establishment of sanctions and consequences in schools, while the obvious object of those actions will be the at-risk individual, an entire culture of prevention is in fact being set forth. That culture will act as a wide prevention measure. In a very real sense, then, intervention as we would have it practiced is prevention as well.

* * * * *

"Enough with the ground work", you say. "Let's get on with how we go about confronting these individuals more effectively. How can we take back control of our families and our classrooms and get some sanity back into our own lives?" Read on!

4: The Interruption Process

What you do need to do
What you do not need to do

We have spent the first three chapters getting ready for what we are going to examine and practice in Chapter 4: the interruption process itself. If this new model is practiced over time, the odds are greatly increased that some significant changes will begin to occur in the irresponsible individual's life. They surely will begin to occur in yours.

The interruption process is designed to accomplish two overriding purposes. First, it is designed to stop the use of tactics; second, it seeks to disrupt the thinking processes with which the irresponsible thinker is comfortable. Note that **these purposes involve our controlling of the interaction**—and perhaps, in a complete change process, our attempt to use this controlled interaction to help the irresponsible person change his or her lifestyle. **They do not involve our direct control of the irresponsible individual**. That is an impossible goal; we cannot make him or her do what we want. Moreover, as we shall suggest, if we could do that, it would not lead to change in the individual. Tempting though it may be, it is therefore actually not desirable as a purpose for the interruption process.

In order to accomplish its purposes, the interruption process will endeavor, as immediate goals, 1) to establish within the specific setting a systematic way of dealing with irresponsible thinking—which will foster a sense of confidence in the interrupter and send a message of consistency to the irresponsible thinker—, 2) to stop the working of thinking errors and tactics long enough to have responsible alternatives offered, and 3) to enable the irresponsible thinker to understand that he or she has the ability to make choices. Interruption may have been best described by a parent whom we trained in this method: she said it was "like throwing a wrench into the gears." Indeed, if we think of the maladaptive thinking patterns and the tactics to avoid accountability as the gears with which the irresponsible behavior is set in motion, then interruption will in fact act as a wrench—to achieve our goals.

One of the things you will do in interruption is to provide choices for the individual with whom you are interacting. He or she may not always make the choices you would like. A part of being effective will be learning to live with their choices. This means, among other things, learning not to take responsibility for their acts.

Scenario 8:

The parents of a boy who is consistently engaging in "small" criminal activity refuse to call in the authorities, saying that they do not want to be responsible for his being taken to jail or to youth detention center. The boy not only continues his criminal behavior outside the house but also becomes more abusive—even physically abusive—at home.

* * * * *

In effect, by accepting responsibility—albeit indirectly—for the child's activity, the parents give him license to expand that activity … to themselves. We will talk more about not taking responsibility for the irresponsible person's actions and hopefully help you become more comfortable with it as a necessary part of an effective interaction.

On another front, it is guaranteed that when you can engage in successful interactions with the irresponsible thinker/s in your life, that life will be less frustrating and what is going on around you will begin to make more sense. Chaos will begin to recede and will be replaced by a sense of direction, purpose, and conviction. You will have an understanding of what you are working with in the irresponsible thinker and what you need to do to make the most effective effort you can to redirect their attention to what their responsibilities are. Most importantly you will understand what you do **not** have to deal with and feel more confident in what you **do** have to deal with. Lastly, remember what you cannot control—which is the fact that other individuals will make their own choices. What you can do is try to help shape the choices and to emphasize the very fact that they have a choice.

What has just been said really amounts to a definition of

what we are calling a "successful" interaction. The individual being held accountable may not feel good when the interaction ends; they may not have got what they wanted; they may feel frustrated and angry. They may, in addition, choose not to do what we would have them do. However, we define "successful" to mean that the interaction will remain respectful, you will remain in control, you will provide the choices and the consequences, and you will leave not feeling frustrated or foolish.

Let's set out a description of the essential parts of such an interruption process:

- Set the agenda (this includes the topic and the expectations)
- Establish common ground
- Don't deal with tactics
- Don't take things personally
- Be prepared to end the interaction
- Provide choices and be prepared to accept the choices that are made
- Stay calm (and use an even tone of voice)[12]

---

[12] For this list of steps in a successful interruption process we have brought together our own experience and some ideas from materials prepared by Koerner and Fawcett, especially sheets entitled "Ways to Interrupt Tactics" and "Seven Guidelines for Controlling Any Meeting and Establishing Rapport."

Let's discuss each of these items, what they mean in general, and what they mean for you specifically.

- First to "set the agenda." By this we mean first that you have it clear in your own mind what the topic of discussion is going to be. Write it down if necessary. You are going to refuse at this time to discuss anything else. You will not discuss whether or not what is happening is fair, whether or not you are a good parent or teacher, whether or not your company has a decent employee policy, etc. You will stay on your selected subject! This will be hard. The individual with whom you are working has everything at stake in moving you off the subject. That is where they will place all of their efforts. This individual is much more comfortable if they can get you to feel defensive and unsure about whether or not you are being fair or unfair as opposed to discussing the fact that the garbage was not taken out, homework was not done, or a part of their job as an employee was left out or not done satisfactorily. An inmate is much more comfortable having the officer who has confronted them get upset in defending whether or not the officer is doing their job properly than having that officer stick to the fact that a rule has been broken and the inmate must be held accountable. Remember, when working with persistently irresponsible thinkers we need to make the effort to understand their thinking and their goals.

An indication of that understanding is to recognize that when these individuals are held accountable they will do everything in their power to throw you off track. Review the tactics now (pp. 43-45), if necessary. Those tactics are going to be used one after another. When one doesn't work, another will be tried. Your effectiveness will depend upon your understanding of what is going on. Being effective at interrupting the irresponsible pattern will require an understanding of the dynamics of this interaction and the willingness to do what you need to do to disrupt the behavior and the thinking. If you are not focused on that task, you will find yourself led astray every time.

- The second part of a successful interaction is to establish common ground. This is a phrase we have all used, but what exactly does it mean? In this context, it means something very basic: that you achieve agreement on at least one thing. "Common ground" generally refers to all of those rules and guidelines that are more or less solidly in place in a discussion between two essentially responsible individuals. As we have said, in a discussion with someone who is predominantly irresponsible some minimal common ground will have to be deliberately and overtly established. It may be that you will ask for a commitment that the two of you treat each other respectfully—indeed, that is the basic fail-safe route to take (see Sample Interaction #5 at the end of this chapter). If the other person is not willing to commit to this, you may want to skip to point five and end the interaction. Even an irresponsible thinker will usually give a commitment that will serve as common ground. (A note: in practice, we do not consider head-nodding or such phrases as "okay, maybe" to constitute a commitment; before going on, we ask the individual either to recite clearly a statement of the common ground agreed upon or, better yet, actually to write that statement down. Without such a commitment, we do not continue the interaction.) Common ground may be more specific than agreement to accord mutual respect. It may be that there will be no yelling. It may be that the entire discussion will take place with you both remaining seated. Or it may be that the discussion will take no longer than 10 minutes, etc. You get the idea. It is important to establish something that you both agree upon and that you be willing to end the discussion if that agreement is not adhered to from that point on.

It is tempting to skip this step. We encourage you not to do so but rather to respect highly its value in a successful interaction with an irresponsible thinker.

It may be that the common ground will not need to be continually restated. It may become something that is automatic, especially if this is an individual with whom you interact frequently. If it is your child, or a student in your classroom, it may be that overtly stating it the first several times will establish a new pattern. But if at any time you lose control of the meeting, we suggest you move back immediately to deliberately establishing common ground. If the other person is not willing to do so, then end the discussion and return to it another time. You will then need to resume establishing common ground with this individual until the fact that there is agreement becomes automatic again.

- The third point is not to deal with tactics. This is the big "NOT" that will make your life easier, but it is really going to test your self-control. Once you experience the value of not responding to tactics, however, you will realize how much energy you have been expending doing just that and only that. How many times have you begun a discussion about responsibility on one topic and ended up discussing another? Or, perhaps ended up discussing nothing at all and just feeling angry and frustrated? This is what tactics are designed to do and what they do very well. They are the behaviors that we end up dealing with rather than the issue at hand. They are the behaviors that drive parents, teachers, employers, and correctional officers to their wits' end. Their ultimate design is either to get the individual seeking accountability off the subject, to divert them to defending themselves instead, to wear them down so that suddenly the main issue is just to get rid of this person, or simply to bring the discussion to an end. Take a good look back at the tactics and be honest: aren't they what we see and hear when we try to hold an irresponsible person responsible for their actions?

Not dealing with tactics is, of course, learning about what you do not have to do. You may accomplish this in several ways. One method would be to familiarize yourself thoroughly with the tactics and then refer to them during an interaction. Perhaps something like the following: "Susie, I see you are choosing to minimize the situation." Or "Jerry, I see you are choosing to remain silent. I can only interpret that as a tactic to avoid the subject, and such tactics are not acceptable." Another approach would be to introduce the tactics ahead of time, if this is an individual with whom you will be interacting often and with whom you typically have frustrating interactions. You may show them a list of the tactics (a parent might wish to stick them up on the refrigerator, for example) and state that from now on you will not deal with them. Then when a discussion begins and tactics come up, you may merely again repeat that you will not deal with tactics, perhaps refer back to the list, and then move back to the point of discussion. Much as with sanctions and consequences and with the rules for the interaction itself, you will in effect be pointing to a pre-established set of rules designating common ground. Especially in institutional settings, the publication of the list of tactics will likely prove valuable. In our own work we use posters that are kept handy, as well as individual handouts (which we reproduce in the Appendices to this book).

The refusal to deal with tactics will, of course, frustrate the irresponsible thinker. You can expect them to switch from one tactic to another to get the conversation back to where they are comfortable—which is having you off balance. Once again, be prepared to end the discussion if the individual is not willing to abandon tactics. Also, it is important to do so in a calm tone of voice and to cast the closure in the terms of the irresponsible individual's choice: "I see that by continually engaging in tactics you have chosen not to go on with the discussion." If you end the discussion abruptly of your own volition without such a statement clarifying the issue of choice, you run the risk of seeming to exercise arbitrary power and most certainly leave yourself open to being badgered on that score. ("Oh, so you can just decide when you want to talk to me…")

You will be accused of being many things when you end an interaction—even after you clarify the issue of choice. You will be called unfair, not understanding, know-it-all, cruel, etc. Stick to your guns. Tactics are not about having a discussion; they are designed to instigate an argument, escalate the stakes, and avoid the main topic. They waste time and, if dealt with, do not help an irresponsible individual learn new thought patterns and behavior. As long as tactics are allowed to go on, interruption and change cannot occur. Understanding what the tactics are and resisting dealing with them will be the single most important thing you do in conserving energy and getting back some control over interactions.

So ... before an interaction you are going to be clear to yourself and the individual you are dealing with about the topic—and the only topic—of discussion, you are going to overtly establish common ground, and you are going to refuse to deal with tactics. This will all become second nature as you continue to practice. On your side of things, at some point you will wonder at all of the tricks and shenanigans you used to go through in a discussion that never ended up dealing with what you had intended anyway. For the irresponsible thinker(s) you deal with, they will begin to realize that you mean what you say and their old thinking and behavior patterns aren't working. Several things can happen at this point, and we will discuss those at some length in Chapter 6. For now, just focus on your effort in the interaction and concentrate on what you need to do and what you don't need to do.

- The next point—namely, that you not take things personally—may sound impossible to achieve. Once again, when you understand what is going on it will not only become possible, you will kick yourself for having wept all the tears over the unkind words and deeds of persistently irresponsible thinkers. If you have a relationship that is important to you and that relationship is based on mutual responsibility, you should definitely be concerned if that individual shows displeasure. However, when you work with an irresponsible thinker the rules are different. Remember back to our discussion about divergent word usage, phrases with different meanings, and the problems an irresponsible thinker and a responsible individual can have in understanding one another. You need to keep these concepts in mind in any interaction.

Whereas a basically responsible individual may never call someone else a name, or do so only under great provocation, an irresponsible thinker will do just about anything and say just about anything to get what they want. The expectation is that this will all be forgotten after the goal has been achieved. This is why you will see demonstrations of anger, or of sadness, that disappear in a flash. We use the term "demonstration of anger" very deliberately. The irresponsible thinker uses the display or demonstration of anger much as a carpenter uses a saw: it is the tool to accomplish the task at hand—and the task is to get what the irresponsible thinker wants at that moment.[13] Anger as an emotion in a basically responsible thinker is, simply, another phenomenon altogether. This is why screams of "I hate you" mean something entirely different out of the mouth of a frustrated adolescent who is not used to being held accountable. What those words mean is "You are in my way"; "You are in the way of what I want." If this child gets what they want, the storm quickly blows over and the sun—a smile—appears. The statement is not really an indication of the child's emotional attachment or feelings.

Trying to keep up with the emotional displays of someone who is determined to get their way is exhausting. If you take literally and personally what

---

[13] We owe the term and concept of "demonstration of anger" to Koerner and Fawcett.

is said and done you will lose your control, your composure, and your power in the interaction. It is important, in order successfully to interrupt an individual who is used to getting away with misbehavior, that you remain in control. Understand that these words and behaviors are the tools of a frustrated, even desperate individual. They are tools that have worked in the past and will not be given up easily. The person, be it a child, student, employee, inmate, etc., will throw anything in your direction that they hope will defeat you. If you take these attacks personally, you will be wounded when you need not be. Rather than wounded you need to be focused, "on task," and matter-of-fact to get through a difficult interaction successfully.

- The fifth point is to be prepared to end the interaction. By this we don't mean that you will each stomp off in opposite directions. Rather, you have set the agenda and are in control of what is the topic for discussion; if the other individual will not comply, be prepared to state in a direct fashion: "I see that you are not willing to stay on the topic (or be respectful, or acknowledge whatever element has been used to construct common ground); you have therefore chosen to end the discussion at this point." Or some such direct statement (we provide some samples below). To persist in a discussion that is lost to tactics, demonstrations of anger, tears, name-calling, etc. is to persist in a useless activity. In fact, it really perpetuates the old patterns. This is what we are trying to avoid.

The illusion we have in keeping a conversation going at all costs is that we thus hold onto the chance of resolving the issue. The problem is that ten times out of ten the issue is no longer being discussed and will not be got back to constructively. The topic has wandered off into another area, most likely one in which the irresponsible individual feels more comfortable (such as argument rather than discussion). The simple fact is that if you both stay on the subject and if tactics are not dealt with, the issues will be being discussed; if not, the issues are not being discussed and therefore cannot be resolved anyway. The model we are introducing will help teach the irresponsible individual how to have a discussion, if he or she chooses to do so.

- The next point on our list is to provide choices and be prepared to accept the choices the individual makes. Initially, this may seem counterintuitive, but in actuality it makes great sense. The goals of structuring interaction this way are both to interrupt irresponsible thinking and behavior and also to encourage the growth of responsible thinking and behavior. Such structuring is going to provide an opportunity for the irresponsible thinker to make choices and to live with the consequences of those choices. Initially, the language of the irresponsible individual avoids acknowledgment of the fact that choices are being made. Your ear will learn to pay close attention to such phrases as: "He made me," "I had to," "What else could I have done?", "I just fell into it." One of the ways we can help irresponsible thinkers take control of their own lives is to give them the language of choice. In so doing, we will find ourselves setting out very clear choices and then understanding that we must let those choices stand.

Let's make one thing clear here. You do not offer a choice with which you cannot live or which is dangerous. But you do offer alternatives and, when the other individual has chosen, you reflect back to them that they have made a choice. For example, you are initiating a discussion with your 17-year-old about using the car. She has abused this privilege in the past, and the consequences of that abuse have previously been established. You make it clear that the topic is about that abuse on her part. As long as that remains the topic of discussion, you continue. Whenever your daughter attempts to change the subject—"Sue's parents never complain about her"—, you steer back to the original topic. You might say something like: "the subject we are discussing is your use of the car in our family." If she returns to that, fine. If not, be prepared to end the conversation. In so doing you can give her an alternative. It might go something like this: "Erica, I am going to give you a choice. You may continue to choose to talk about something other than your use of the car, in which case we will end this conversation and leave the issue unresolved. You understand that there will be no further use of the car [which is a pre-established consequence] until we reach an agreement. Or, you may stay on the topic and we can continue to discuss this problem to see if we can reach an agreement." She now has a choice, and with that choice comes a specific consequence. This is when it will be important for you not to deal with tactics. Erica will want to attack you with something she doesn't like about you as a parent. She may want to talk about the few times when she did not abuse the privilege of using the car, or some such topic. You will refuse to get off into those dead ends. You will point out that she is choosing to avoid the subject and then end conversation for now. You are now done with this interaction. You may wish to set up another time when she agrees to be more open to discussing the topic at hand. On the other hand, she has the choice of staying on the subject and working on the issue.

When you set out these alternatives and make the consequences clear ahead of time, you are really helping that individual uncover the fact that they are making choices every day of their lives. They truly may not be aware of this. Part of observing the structure we recommend is that we begin to give this individual the language of choice. We help remove the language of helplessness and blame. We always have choices. They may not be ones we like, but we always have them. An important step towards taking responsibility for our lives is to accept this fact and knowingly utilize the ability to choose.

- Our last guideline reads "stay calm". Actually it reads "**stay calm.**" "Yeah, sure," you say. "I am supposed to stay calm and speak matter-of-factly in the face of someone who may be yelling at me, calling me names, shedding tears, threatening me, etc." Yes, you are—if you choose to be effective. Remembering not to take things personally will be critical to the goal of staying calm. Remember that you stand in the way of what this person wants. That is the usual source—and usually the only source—of the abuse directed your way. Staying calm may require some practice, but it is a realistic goal. If, however, you have set an agenda, established common ground, are refusing to deal with tactics, realize that you don't need to take what is being said personally, and are prepared to end the discussion if necessary, staying calm and speaking in a calm tone of voice are not going to constitute the enormous task you might imagine. Committing yourself not to deal with tactics alone will tend to keep you calm. Focusing on what you need to do to offer choices and indicate consequences will help keep you rational and focused on your thinking process as well as on the thinking of the irresponsible individual you are confronting. In other words, if you are committed to following the structure we have set out, staying calm will merely be another part of that structure.

As with any other skill, the more you follow this model the better you will get at it and the more natural it will feel. If at first it doesn't go well, try it again next time. It will work. Remind yourself that your effectiveness goes down as your anger goes up. Your ability to be effective diminishes as your feelings take the lead and you abandon your own thought processes. The more thoughtful you can remain in the midst of difficult interactions, the more effective you will be. And above all, remind yourself of what these interactions have been like in the past. Were **they** effective? Did **they** accomplish anything in the way of problem-solving? Remember how upset and exhausted you were after each such interaction. Remember the madness. Then trust us: this is a way to end that madness.

Below we provide some sample interactions for a variety of settings. Use them for practice. Find your own words and your own comfort with them. Don't be afraid to rehearse before you begin. We all do that with the things we care about and want to do well. It is appropriate that you would want to bring that same effort to learning how to work effectively with your students, your children, or your employees. When you see the magic in learning to put the above steps into practice, your life as, say, a correctional officer will change substantially. You will find yourself going home with more energy. You will spend less time in frustrating and repetitive interactions with the inmates. As a counselor, you will find yourself understanding that you don't have to explain everything. You will more readily be able to identify those questions which are asked merely to keep you busy. You will find your time in therapy sessions spent more effectively. You will be learning a skill that is extremely effective in respectfully cutting through denial in your clients. We ourselves have used these techniques in all of the above-mentioned settings and found them incredibly effective.

Now take a look at some of the examples below.

Sample Interactions

All attempts by the individual being held accountable to use tactics and divert the focus of the discussion are **politely** ignored. Remain focused on **your** task. Strive to relay to the individual in a calm and respectful manner that tactics will not be dealt with and decision-making is expected.

1. A meeting with a purpose

"_____ (individual's name), our purpose today is to get you enrolled in school."

If they cooperate—fine. If not:

"_____ (name), your choices are to cooperate in getting signed up for school, the consequences of which are that you can move ahead and hopefully complete the GED as you want to do. Or you may choose not to cooperate. The consequences of that choice are that we will end our meeting and you will not be enrolled in school."

"You may choose to reschedule if you like."

2. Dealing with someone being rude or disruptive in class

"_____ , you are disrupting the class (being rude to me, being rude to the class). You may choose to stop being disruptive, the consequences of which are that we can all go on learning, or you may choose to continue. The consequences of choosing to be disruptive are that you will have to leave the classroom and you will not be able to continue on toward the GED.

3. Dealing with someone being rude or disruptive in class

"_____ , our purpose here is to learn math. You may choose to cooperate, the consequences of which are that you may continue learning math, or you may choose to continue to disrupt the class. The consequences then are that you will have to leave the class and you will not learn math, which is required for graduation.

4. Dealing with the use of silence as a tactic

"_____ , I see that you have chosen not to participate with me in the discussion. I do not deal with tactics. You are choosing not to cooperate and the consequences are that you will have to leave the classroom. If you choose to return, please bring with you a written statement addressing how things will be different in the future. The consequences of choosing to return are that you may continue to learn English and move on toward completion of the GED."

5. A meeting with an uncooperative individual

"_____ , I am willing to do whatever it takes to give you respect. Are you willing to do the same?"

Continue to repeat this calmly while looking directly at the individual. They may choose to leave. Point out that they are making a choice to leave and what the consequences are. More commonly, they will agree to what you are asking. If you are in a setting in which you can then ask them to write the statement down on a sheet of paper, that would be helpful in making the commitment concrete. Then move on to what the purpose of your meeting or interaction is: enroll the student, move to your office to talk, etc.

To be sure, the language we are using here tends toward the formal and repeats similar phrases. We encourage you to find the level with which you are comfortable. Bear in mind, however, that there is considerable value in being at least slightly formulaic. It works well to have a few set phrases that can be used in various contexts. If you construct your statements around such phrases, not only will you ensure that you will be using the language of choice in each interaction and find it easier to maintain a matter-of-fact tone but you also will be sending out some important signals: that you are being clear, even-handed, and consistent (reeducation depends, in part, on consistency and repetition) and that what you are saying is part of a wider undertaking. Interaction phrased in this manner will also tend to undercut the irresponsible thinker's likely argument that what is happening to them is arbitrary and unrelated to their thinking/behavior choices.

6. A discussion between parent and child

"Harry, I want to talk about the fact that your chores are not being done. That will be the topic of our conversation."

If Harry cooperates—fine. If not:

"Harry, you are choosing not to stay on the subject of our conversation (or not paying attention, or using silence as a tactic). The consequences of that have already been laid out. You will not be able to go out with your friends until the chores are done. If you choose to go on with this discussion we can talk about the chores and try to reach an understanding.

Remember, be prepared to follow through on consequences!

7. An angry inmate in a correctional setting

"Hey, officer, I thought you said you were going to find out my court date".

"James, I said I would look that up if I had time."

The officer is now done with the exchange. James may call him names and continue to yell and attempt to harass him. The officer does not have to deal with James's tactics, which under the circumstances might, for example, involve attacking his competency: "Hey, how'd you get to wear that uniform. You aren't smart enough to add two and two." Or the inmate might try introducing irrelevant material such as calling him racist or saying something like "you are always picking on me." If the officer tries to defend himself, he puts himself just where the inmate wants him. If the officer can be pulled into an argument, the excitement in the whole cell block goes up. More name-calling and baiting follow. The point is that if the officer refuses to be drawn into further discussion and goes on about his duties in a calm manner, James will give up. There will be no excitement and thus no interest in pursuing the officer. Not only that, but over time other inmates will get the word that "you can't rile so-and-so." The excitement of possibly being able to upset that officer will have disappeared. That correctional officer really can choose to avoid what would be a fruitless, repetitive, and frustrating exchange.

8. An employer confronting an employee who is repeatedly late

"Janice, your supervisor tells me that you have repeatedly been late to work and that this problem has been brought to your attention several times."

If Janice cooperates with this discussion—fine. If not:

Let's say Janice wants to talk about car trouble, or domestic problems, or the inefficient bus schedule. (The important point to remember here is that we are addressing a pattern. If Janice is a responsible employee who has had car trouble this week, that is approached differently than if Janice has shown a pattern of irresponsible behavior at work.) The employer would restate the purpose of the discussion and refuse to talk about the other issues. Janice's task is to get to work on time and that is the focus of the discussion. If Janice continues to avoid her responsibility—and the topic of discussion—, the employer needs to be prepared to end the conversation. In so doing he may offer her some choices: "Janice, we may continue this conversation about your repeatedly being late for work and focus on your responsibility to be punctual. Then perhaps we can resolve the issue and you can return to work. If you choose to speak about other issues, I will end the conversation. The result of this choice on your part will be that the subject of your being late remains unresolved. As a result, I may well have to terminate you as an employee".

* * * * *

These are examples from different areas of life involving different professions. The basic principles are the same. They are expressed in the points listed earlier in this chapter.

Let's now go back to the scenario with which we began this book and see how Mr. Pierson might have handled the situation if he knew what we know now.

Scenario 1
Second Version:

As Jimmy enters the classroom he tosses some trash in the direction of the waste basket and then meanders on to his seat. The wadded-up papers scatter on the floor. Mr. Pierson, the 9th-grade teacher, looks up from his desk, stands up, and walks over to the scattered trash.

Mr. Pierson: "Jim! Pick this up please."

Jimmy: "You gonna make me?"

Mr. Pierson: "Jim, you know the rules. You can pick up the paper, take your seat, and continue to be a part of the math class, or you can choose to leave the paper on the floor. The consequences of that are that you will be asked to leave and you will no longer be taking math.

(Jimmy will likely look around for support from his classmates and continue to berate Mr. Pierson.)

Mr. Pierson: "Jim, I've said all I'm going to say; the choice is yours." (He returns to regular class work.)

* * * * *

Note the several desirable features of the use of the interruption techniques. 1) Jimmy is reminded of preestablished rules, so no elaborate discussion about common ground has to take place. 2) Consequences are preestablished and can be pointed to immediately and definitively. 3) The consequences themselves are immediate. 4) A choice is formulated within a clear context of sanctions and consequences. 5) The choice is presented to

Jimmy and left up to him. 6) The potential for excitement and disruption within the class that Jimmy's behavior and verbal tactics represent is diffused by Mr. Pierson's handling of the situation. 7) The entire incident demonstrates to the other students that the rules and their application are consistent. It thus functions not only as an intervention in the case of Jimmy but also in a preventive manner with the rest of the class.

* * * * *

Now let's move on to Chapter 5 and take a look at ourselves as an important ingredient in these interactions. In the presentations and workshops we have done, this topic often ends up being the most popular and most meaningful for participants. What can we learn about ourselves that will affect the kind of interactions that we will tend to have? And how will what we know about ourselves impact our effectiveness?

5: Know Your Own Thinking Errors and Vulnerabilities

First of all, as we have said before, we all use thinking errors and tactics. It is the extent to which we use them and their pattern that defines their impact in our lives. Let's look at an example of what we mean.

Say you lead a basically responsible life. You take care of your responsibilities, the bills get paid, errands get run, tasks somehow get done, etc. Now, let's also say that one day you find yourself feeling particularly overwhelmed with your responsibilities and feeling very tired. You think, "I would really like some time to myself." So you call in to work and say you are sick. You take the day off, relax, catch up on some sleep. You return to work the following day, feeling refreshed and ready to get back into the rhythm of your life. Two weeks later you feel the same way and, remembering what a nice day you had, you call in sick again and make up an excuse for your supervisor. What if this begins to become a pattern? Whereas two months ago you would not have thought of lying about your health, now you begin to do so frequently. Pretty soon your co-workers begin to ask you about your health, and you tell some more lies. You run out of sick leave and still keep up the practice, but now your paycheck is smaller and some bills are not getting paid. "To heck with them" you tell yourself. "I worked my tail off for the past year and never heard a word of thanks. They can just do without me now and then." You see what is beginning to happen? You are beginning to use more and more of the thinking errors and to use them more often. They are becoming comfortable. Discomfort is dealt with by using more errors (feeling victimized, blaming others, seeing yourself as responsible despite yours actions to the contrary) and more tactics (putting others down as justification for your own actions, minimizing, etc.).

If this individual keeps up this lifestyle, their life will begin to reflect the changes in the choices being made. More and more irresponsible behavior will be demonstrated, followed by more excuses, anger, and resentment. This individual may get fired, or may quit in a fit of anger.

But, let's go back to our original scenario. What if this person called in sick for a day off but then, after returning to work, decided that, while that may have been the way they chose to solve the problem of fatigue and feeling overwhelmed this time, they feel uncomfortable doing it again? This is an example of someone who uses the errors and tactics but also self-corrects. This person may say to him- or herself something like the following: "I can't go on lying about my health. If I am overburdened, I need to handle it in a different way. Maybe by taking a look at letting some things go, being more efficient with my time, or, perhaps, making a schedule for myself and taking a look at time I may be wasting." You see the difference? It is not the presence or absence of maladaptive thinking patterns that defines responsibility, it is the pattern of their use. We are all susceptible to them. Moreover, it is usually the case that each of us is more susceptible to some of them than to others.

Why don't you take a moment to look over the thinking errors listed in Chapter 1, and select the three that you think you use the most often. We will now spend some time looking at what your identifications may mean.

The purpose of this exercise is for each of us to look for his or her own vulnerabilities. What are your weaknesses? In what ways are you susceptible to being manipulated? The point of carefully going through this self-examination ahead of time is that you will know what you need to work especially hard to be aware of when you deal with irresponsible thinkers. You will know the most likely ways that you can be hurt, manipulated, or conned by such individuals. Let's get more specific.

What if your "top three" thinking errors were victimscript, unrealistic self-image, and specialness? This is not information that should cause you to throw in the towel. It is instead excellent information for alerting you to ways in which you need to be cautious. Your tendencies are going to be to feel sorry for yourself and also more easily to fall victim to feeling sorry for others. Secondly, you will tend to want to see yourself and your motives through rose-colored glasses: you are special, and especially good, or clever, or intuitive, or what-have-you. You will be easily molded by an individual who tells you that you are the best counselor they have ever had. Or that they have never been able to talk to anyone as understanding as you before. You will be the parent to whom the child says: "I can't talk to _____ like I can talk to you." Approached the right way, you could end up being like silly putty to someone whose goal is to avoid accountability. You may be the individual who willingly goes to bat for this individual rather than putting that same energy into consistently holding them accountable. We all wear the ways we can be manipulated on our sleeves, to be easily used and exploited by the individual willing to do just that. We give them the information on how we can easily be manipulated and "got off their backs." It is our job, if we do not want to become part of the problem, to be aware of how we are likely to be used and to be alert in order to avoid that outcome.

Something else may be hard for you: being consistent in holding someone accountable. Holding someone accountable, especially someone who has got away over time with being irresponsible, will not make that person happy. If you like to think of yourself as always helping others, and if that category means making other people feel good, working with the irresponsible thinker will be a challenge. When you step up to interrupt the irresponsible pattern using the model we suggest, the irresponsible thinker is going to feel frustrated and angry, and you are the one they will blame. It will take some courage on your part—and understanding that this is what needs to be done—to address effectively the behavior and the thinking that underlies that behavior. We can worry about feelings later, when the individual has made some changes in thinking.

What about some of the other maladaptive thinking patterns? Say your top three come up as specialness, control through power, and sense of entitlement. It should not take a rocket scientist to foresee that your vulnerabilities will center around getting into power struggles. One of the keys of the model we are suggesting is that it is designed to avoid exactly that. Power struggles are where the irresponsible individual is most comfortable. He or she strives to put all issues on a competitive basis. This is the child or adult with whom it is very difficult to have a discussion but extremely easy to have an argument, and an argument with an irresponsible person will be a dance in tactics. Before you can count to three, you and the individual you are working with, be it your son or daughter, a student, a correctional client, or an employee, will be running through the tactics to avoid accountability until one of you gets tired and quits. Who do you bet that will be? The worst part about this scenario is that the original purpose of the discussion will have been lost in the ensuing competition. Your struggle will be to stick to the steps set out in the model NO MATTER WHAT.

Your efficiency will go up as your anger and frustration go down. Staying calm will be your goal.

In addition to simply staying calm on the surface, you are going to need to summon up a helping of "humble pie" to combat the implications of your sense of specialness, especially your tendency to want to "go it alone." Look to what we all have in common. Admit that working effectively with an irresponsible thinker takes planning and team work. Keep in mind that closing the loop is an important part of addressing such thinking and behavior effectively.

Scenario 9:

In a family the father's two dominant errors are specialness and unrealistic self-image; the mother's are control through power and sense of entitlement. They have difficulty holding their daughter accountable for her behavior. It turns out that the daughter's strategy is as follows: when the mother tries to hold her accountable, she (the daughter) initiates a power struggle, and the mother, vulnerable in that area, falls right in. Normally, when the yelling reaches a certain level, both storm out of the room. The daughter then goes to the father and tells him that he is the only person who understands her, the only one she can really talk to, etc. The daughter thus escapes accountability for her behavior and in fact controls the household through this manipulation of her parents.

* * * * *

The two primary things needed here, of course, are first the parents' awareness of their own vulnerabilities and work to minimize them and then a commitment to closing the loop in the home environment with their daughter.

Let's look at some more potential combinations. What about inappropriate expectations, unrealistic self-image, and victimscript? How will these errors tend to subvert your effectiveness as a parent, as a helping professional, or as an employer with personnel problems? First of all, you may tend to want to ignore the problem. You may find yourself continually in favor of the path of least resistance. Or, you may tend to quit when the going gets tough. Let someone else handle this; appease this individual and pass him or her and all their problems on to the next guy. Or, perhaps, that isn't your style, but you are instead a briber. By that we mean you avoid the task of holding the individual accountable by finding out what they want and making a deal (remember Scenario #7 and the parents who bought the special shoes!). Risking and taking a chance on something new may be a particular challenge. This might mean, among other things, that you will find it exceedingly difficult to give the models and concepts we are presenting in this book a try. To risk something new and perhaps not do a good job initially, or not get the results you want, may be threatening enough possibilities that you will abandon the attempt altogether. You might decide to stick with what you are doing, even though you don't like the results and know that you often end the day frustrated.

As well as being hampered by the dangers that you see in the risk-taking involved in trying out a new and perhaps foreign set of orientations and methods, you will have a strong need to be looked at appreciatively as well as a tendency to feel picked on. We would suggest that you need to pay particular attention to interruption step 4, namely not to take things personally. You may get your feelings wounded and want to give in. You may feel resentful at having to go through a model that clearly makes it a point of importance not to give an angry individual what he or she wants at the moment. You will wonder "Isn't there an easier way to do this and have everyone feel better?" Initially, you will have to remind yourself "No, there really isn't." Not when you are trying to interrupt a pattern of irresponsible thinking and behavior. What you can remind yourself of is that when you begin to see how well this model works and how effective it is in helping these individuals understand the value of choice, you will indeed feel better about yourself. You will feel a sense of power in that efficacy, and you will experience the thrill of having had the courage to try something that was uniquely focused on what that individual needed for help rather than on your own vulnerability patterns. This is a hard lesson and one that takes a lot of honesty to admit and accept.

The fact is—and this is the last time we'll say it—the systems we design are often more about our own needs for comfort than about effectively interacting with those having trouble. Our own vulnerabilities needn't rule us out in this task, but it is helpful in increasing our effectiveness as a parent, a teacher, a counselor, an employer, or perhaps someone working in the field of corrections to know ourselves well and know what advantages, disadvantages, and propensities we ourselves bring to an interaction.

How about one last example that involves closed thinking? Let's suppose that closed thinking is paired up with sense of entitlement and control through power. What are the vulnerabilities it would be helpful for you to be aware of?

Closed thinking will prompt you to think that you "know it all." You may tend to be rigid or inflexible because you don't take in new information easily. You may also have difficulty being a good team player in that you will hold back information that tends to give you the upper hand or some possible advantage in a future situation. You may be difficult as a co-worker because taking criticism is hard for you. Being self-critical may be even harder. When control through power and sense of entitlement team up together, they are powerful allies.

Sense of entitlement will make it very difficult for you to ease back on controlling the outcome and allow others to make their own choices. It might also be a part of your own thinking and behavior to feel that your way is always the best way. When you put this together with a tendency to use power for purposes of control, you could be the worst kind of "I told you so" parent or co-worker. You likely will have a tendency to get involved in struggles over "outcome." You will want to fight over and try to control how things turn out, then not want to listen to other possibilities or other suggestions. You may find it difficult to listen to interpretations with which you don't agree. You may well find the model we have set forth a heady challenge, for it seems to be asking you to "give up control." You may feel as if you are going into an interaction without any power. We suggest that you will find that such is not the case. If you give this model a fair chance, you will discover that there is in fact a great deal of power in it, but the power is about its effect on the irresponsible individual. Use of the interruption process we describe will take the focus off your need to be in charge of the information, the outcome, and your ability to make that outcome happen; indeed it will relieve you of that enormous responsibility. The interaction will be less about you and more about an effective system of interrupting an irresponsible thinker and helping them learn to make different choices. What you are going to focus on is providing a topic for a discussion that will take place in a calm atmosphere, one in which choices will be offered and made and consequences enforced.

We could continue with many more combinations of susceptibilities, but by now you have the idea. What this inventory of errors and speculation about their effects does is to help you learn about yourself—so that you can lessen your vulnerability and thereby increase your effectiveness. This in turn will free up much of the energy that is currently going into trying to defeat the tactics the irresponsible thinker is directing at you—tactics designed to affect you in the areas where your principal thinking errors make you the most susceptible. Before any of us undertakes an effort in which we want to succeed, we all need to know our weaknesses as well as our strengths. It is in that awareness that we develop strength.

You can be certain that the irresponsible individual with whom you are interacting is working to analyze your vulnerabilities. Discerning what someone particularly cares about or prides himself or herself on and knowing how to upset or con that person by playing to those vulnerabilities are parts of their operating procedure in the use of tactics. An important element in effectively employing the model we suggest thus comes in knowing your potential "weak spots" ahead of time and acting accordingly. Your willingness to fact-find about yourself and to look at how your propensities can undermine your effectiveness in working with irresponsible thinkers is a good gauge of your understanding of what is needed to have a successful interaction. If such an interaction is repeatedly contaminated or derailed because of your lack of self-knowledge, you will want to work harder to prepare yourself.

6: What to Expect

So, you have read this far and what we have said has made enough sense to you that you are seriously considering trying the interruption process at home, at work, perhaps with a client you are counseling, or on your job as a correctional officer. Maybe you have some personnel problems in your office that you are thinking of addressing differently. Perhaps you work in a treatment facility for adolescents and what we have said rings true to you. You see the appropriateness of the approach for the youngsters with whom you work. As you read this book, you have been paying more attention to what is going on around you at home and in other settings and you begin to see and recognize the maladaptive thinking patterns that we have mentioned. You have become aware of the tactics to avoid being held accountable and begin to recognize how much time out of your day is spent in fielding them rather than in problem-solving. Maybe you have grown so good at recognizing tactics that you have watched as a friend or a co-worker gets hopelessly caught up in them. As you watch, you see the interaction move away from the original subject and wander off into a swamp of accusations and self-defense maneuvers that take on a life of their own. You are curious or even anxious to give the interruption process a try, but perhaps, as with anything new, you are wondering what to expect. We all know there is no miracle cure for the problems we are addressing, or we would not have been struggling year after year to little or no avail with irresponsible thinkers. Let us try to set out what we see as appropriate expectations based on our own experiences in using and teaching this interruption process.

The first appropriate expectation we would list is for you to be prepared to use lots and lots of repetition. Consistency and repetition will be your most effective and powerful tools. You will be tested again and again by the individuals with whom you are using this interruption process to see if you really mean it. "Are you really serious about this?" "Is this a permanent change, or is it just a phase?" So, first of all, expect to be challenged by the individual/s with whom you are working and understand you will need to be prepared to demonstrate that you are committed to the long haul. At some point, the individual will likely realize that tactics won't be effective in their getting what they want. The discussion will then become more subdued and will focus more consistently on the desired topic. This may or may not indicate some degree of change, but it surely does signal a new basis for interaction. It is possible that more communication can now take place—which is the first step to a number of possible outcomes: you may well see a lessening, or outright elimination, of the problems that caused you to engage in the interruption process with this irresponsible thinker in the first place; you may see that individual engage in a wider attempt to redo their life; you may wish to help them build on their first steps by following up with a more elaborate reeducation plan for them.

A word of encouragement: do not be dissuaded by the knowledge that others in your household, agency, or community may be doing other things—or nothing at all—with irresponsible thinkers. "Closing the loop" is an important goal, but we, for example, see significant results with individuals who come to us weekly and, as far as we can determine, get no reinforcing support outside of the groups. We are of the impression (and it is just that, an impression with, as of yet, no data to back it up) that the extent to which the irresponsible patterns have become entrenched in the individual and the degree of his or her motivation for change are key factors in determining the results that can be obtained.

All of this leads us to mention a second appropriate expectation: you may legitimately expect to experience less frustration and fewer feelings of hopelessness. You will certainly begin to experience less anger. You will also stop doing all of that "explaining." (We remember one exhausted counselor who worked with adolescents saying with relief: "Oh, I thought I had to explain **everything**.") When you are confronted with tactics, that is exactly what you should **not** be doing. As you take control of the interaction, you will begin to take back control of family, classroom, etc.

If you follow the guidelines we suggest for a successful interaction you will achieve one key goal: you will shift the discomfort and responsibility back onto the irresponsible individual. This, of course, is where it belongs. Without this sort of clear message, the persistently irresponsible individual will slide on through life using the tactics as a shield to avoid the consequences of his or her choices. This is not helpful to any of us. It keeps the irresponsible individual from learning the lessons and making the connections necessary to promote more responsible decision-making. In addition, it continues the cycle of mutual anger and recrimination. It adds fuel to a fire we should be working to put out.

Something else: you should be prepared for things to get worse before they get better. Oh no! This sounds discouraging! We understand that initially this is not good news, but DON'T DESPAIR and DON'T GIVE UP! It is to be expected that in initiating a process that increases the discomfort of the irresponsible individual you will be initiating a process that will **not** go unnoticed. This individual will want to demonstrate that discomfort. That may mean demonstrating anger (about "demonstration of anger," see pp. 93-94) and/or escalating the use of tactics. It may mean he or she will use more abusive language. A student may complain about you as a teacher and try to be removed from your classroom. These are expectable reactions. In rare cases, the irresponsible thinker may resort to violence. Violence should be dealt with appropriately—that is, through the use of previously-determined sanctions and consequences (according to the circumstances, calling the school discipline officer, the security guards, the police, etc.). The demonstration of their discomfort may mean that this individual will want to put as much distance as possible between you and them. If you are a parent using this technique, it might mean that your son or daughter will initially run away. (We have worked with families where children have chosen to move out, often to a friend's home, as a part of demonstrating discomfort. Interventions involve change and thus put pressures of various sorts on the whole family. Remember, individuals may make choices that disappoint us.) This is a test of your determination and trust in this approach. Anyone who has grown used to not being held accountable is going to feel very uncomfortable with choices and consequences.

Once again we would ask you: "Compare these expectable reactions to your current situation." For example, you may already be living with similar behaviors. You may have become used to a kind of chaos or a level of abuse that has been gradually escalating—and will simply continue to do so if the problem is not addressed differently. You may have slipped into a pattern of letting things slide and not confronting issues out of anxiety at the thought of the scene that will inevitably ensue. So your situation does not improve and you move from one demand or argument to the next, settling for anything that will end the conflict of the moment. We ask you to take an honest look at what you are currently experiencing using a variety of the standard approaches we have all tried again and again. These include being understanding, using appeasement or bribery, and the use of power, either verbal or physical. If you have picked up this book, been intrigued, and read up to this point, we suggest that you **are** looking for something new and more effective. You may have bought this book for your neighbor, but part-way through began to see some uses in your own life. Your interest may fall somewhere between mere curiosity and full-blown necessity. Whatever your situation, we strongly encourage you to give this approach a try.

We have mentioned earlier in the book that some individuals, when they have choices, will continue to make choices that disappoint us. Some of the individuals with whom we work will continue to be irresponsible. This is sad. This is not what we work for, but we do need to understand that we cannot prevent this outcome. We can do our job as effectively as we can. We can understand the irresponsible individual and his or her thinking. We can understand the purpose of the tactics and choose not to respond to them. We can be willing to be consistent, knowing that that is what is needed, and understand that we still may not be able to help bring about change in the individuals with whom we are interacting. We can offer choices so that they will be able to fashion a more responsible lifestyle. But remember: we have to let them make those choices—even the choice not to change. For a parent this is painful indeed. More painful than it will be for an employer who uses this approach and then accepts that an employee who continues to think irresponsibly will have to be let go. Different relationships and levels of involvement will bring different levels of sadness and suffering for those who watch individuals choose to continue on with irresponsible thinking and irresponsible behavior. The message we have tried to share in these pages has focused on the benefits of changing the nature of each interaction. A respectful interaction that uses the language of choice has value in itself. This value we believe worthwhile, whether or not the outcome desired—the making of more responsible choices—is always the one achieved. It is our experience, however—and that of the significant majority of the people with whom we have worked—that progress will be made with this approach more surely and consistently than with any other now being practiced.

Afterword: Extensions and Applications—Widening the Focus

We would not like to close without encouraging you to think about the extensions that exist for the concept and method of interruption we have presented in this short book and also about the wide variety of applications to which it can be put. The particular case you are dealing with may not relate neatly to any of those we have presented, and it is important to us that you see all that can be done with this approach.

First of all, in the preceding pages we have been careful to differentiate interruption from change, having it as our present purpose merely to deal with the first of them. As you can see, however, the dividing line is not always a clear one. Moreover, what if your complete goal is not only to achieve the benefits that come from interruption? What if what you ultimately desire is to effect basic change in the irresponsible thinker with whom you are dealing? Well, interruption is the first step in a program for such change. Indeed, it is not far from the mark to say that change is brought about through interruption after interruption after interruption—within, to be sure, a wide program of reeducation. A warning, however. While the method of interruption will remain the same even when it is used in a total change program (that is, the steps will continue to be the same), sometimes its strategy will be different, especially after the initial stages of interruption have passed. Let's go back a third and last time to Jimmy and Mr. Pierson in that 9th-grade classroom, assuming now that Mr. Pierson is a dedicated and knowledgeable change agent.

Scenario 1
Third Version:

As Jimmy enters the classroom he tosses some trash in the direction of the waste basket and then meanders on to his seat. The wadded-up papers scatter on the floor. Mr. Pierson, the 9th-grade teacher, looks up from his desk, stands up, and walks over to the scattered trash.

Mr. Pierson: "Jim! Pick this up please."

Jimmy: "You gonna make me?"

Mr. Pierson (after a pause): "Jim, do you mind if I pick it up? (He picks up the trash and puts it in the waste basket.) Now, would you be willing to look at what you were thinking that caused you to choose to come into the classroom that way?" (And/or "Would you be willing to look at the thinking errors [and tactics] that caused you to choose to come into the classroom that way?") (And/or "Would you be willing to write a thinking report on the thinking errors [and tactics] that caused you to choose to come into the classroom that way?")

* * * * *

In this version the goals have changed. It is also the case that Jimmy and Mr. Pierson now have much more common ground established—presumably as the result of having undergone many interactions like that in the second version of this scenario [pp. 111-112]). Mr. Pierson is now trying to get Jimmy himself to analyze and come to grips with his thinking patterns. Therefore, he picks up the trash himself, both in order to defuse the situation with Jimmy and with the rest of the class and also in order to shift focus away from the single incident and onto Jimmy's thinking pattern. There is of course much more than that involved: the language of choice, staying calm and using a matter-of-fact tone of voice, etc. We bring you this final version of the example merely to help you understand the implications and uses of the interruption process: it has great value in and of itself, but it can also be a primary vehicle and requisite first step in a more thoroughgoing and profound change process, and it will thus vary somewhat according to the specific context in which it is being used.

This approach, then—the constructing of interactions in a way that employs the language of choice and the use of consequences—, does have the potential to promote basic change. Reaching that goal, however—especially with the entrenched irresponsible thinker—, usually requires that interruption be supported by a reeducation plan, group work, individual study (that is, homework), and support groups. Through such means we, for example, seek to instill in the irresponsible thinker a series of "responsible replacements" for the maladaptive thinking patterns. Also to that end, we have designed a list of questions that address each thinking error in turn and suggest responsible replacements for it (see the Appendices to this book). We use that list right next to the list of the maladaptive thinking patterns and refer to it in interacting with our clients.

Under such a regimen (which is what we seek to provide in the programs that we implement), we see many individuals, starting with interruption, develop respectful interactions and better relationships. We see the ability to have better relationships expand into a willingness to be held accountable and also into a wider vision of change, to gradually encompass responsible living skills. We do see some people fashion a whole responsible value system. This is change is its broadest sense. The focus of this book, however, has been on bringing some purpose and sanity back into the interactions the most of us have with persistently irresponsible individuals. The next step, that of basic change, usually requires the presence of someone with professional training or, at least, supervision by such a person. But interruption as it is outlined here is the requisite first step, and it will "stop the madness."

As regards applications, we have introduced this approach to various kinds of groups. We ourselves use it in individual and group counseling. We also teach this approach in our parent education groups. We have trained individuals and groups who intend to use the approach in a variety of settings including education, social services, mental health, and corrections. We have spent as little as fifteen minutes at public meetings trying to share what we have talked about throughout this book and spent up to four days with those groups who are training for certification in its use. We have found the information to be flexible within different structures. We have re-designed entire systems in some organizations, but in other situations this approach has been merged into the existing structure.

The approach is also expandable. You may choose to use

it yourself in individual interactions in your personal life, you may use it in groups—for example, several counselors or teachers working together within a program or a school—, or it may be adopted as a management strategy agency- or company-wide. (To return quickly to our discussion of intervention/prevention in Chapter 3, we would observe that it will have a strong preventive force when deployed in virtually any institution.) It is applicable in homes, schools and classrooms, community programs, treatment centers, mental health agencies, businesses, group homes, correctional institutions, police departments, as well as in probation and parole. It is suitable to interactions between parent and child, adult and adult, teacher and student, counselor and client, employer and employee, parole officer and parolee, etc. This approach to interruption of irresponsible thinking and behavior can be implemented in units as small as a household and as large as a community. The benefits will grow accordingly.

Imagine…

Appendices

Maladaptive Thinking Patterns

<u>Victimscript</u>. Individual persistently blames others including family, friends, social conditions, etc:
> Language often indicative of this pattern:
> - "I couldn't help it. You know where I live."
> - "There's no getting along with that teacher."

<u>Unrealistic self-image</u>. Sees self as responsible despite actions:
> - "Hey, I'm not a bad person. You act like this is a nuclear war."
> - "Can anyone who can paint like this be all bad?"

Closed thinking. Unwilling to listen, to share information, or to be self-critical; goes on assumptions; lies, more likely by omission than by commission:

- "You're bogus. I suppose you think you know it all."
- "Why is this always about me?"

Sense of entitlement that extends to persons, places, and things; thoughts of intense jealousy:

- "Hey, she left it laying around didn't she? What did she expect me to do, leave it alone?"
- "He's got insurance."

Compartmentalized thinking. What happened before doesn't count, what happens now does not affect the future; what they want they want now. Little sense that behavior has consequences:

- "So what's your problem; I said I was sorry didn't I?"
- "I knew you'd bring that up; that was last year."
- "I won't get caught."

Inappropriate expectations about life that lead to boredom, an unwillingness to appreciate daily effort, and/or unreasonable fears:
- "I can't do it." (I.e., "I'm not willing to try.")
- "I can't get a job." (I.e., "I can't get the job I want.")
- "I can't believe this grade. It isn't fair. I stayed up all night for that test."

Control through power. Expects to be able to control situations and other individuals; uses manipulation and intimidation to achieve this goal; uses sex for power and control rather than for intimacy.
- "He made me hit him. He wouldn't do what I said."
- "I said 'now' and I meant it!"
- "I don't feel like it. Make me."

Specialness. A sense of being superior or unique; conviction that they are living in a "natural" state while "artificial" rules are for others:
- "Ten years to become a doctor? I can do it in four easy!"

Questions That Lead to Responsible Choices

Victimscript:

- What was my part?
- Am I willing to be held accountable?
- Am I willing to use "I" language?
- Am I willing to talk about choices I am making now?

Unrealistic self-image:

- Have I thought about how I am affecting others?
- Is this how I would want to be treated?
- Have I asked for feedback from someone responsible?

Closed Thinking:

- Have I told it all?
- Am I prepared to admit when I am wrong?
- Am I willing to listen when it is uncomfortable?
- Do I know all the facts?

Sense of entitlement:
- Have I asked myself what is the responsible thing to do?
- Am I honoring my commitment to change?
- Have I done whatever it takes?

Compartmentalized thinking:
- Am I focused on my effort rather than on solely controlling the outcome?
- Am I thinking ahead?
- Am I acting from feelings or from thinking?

Inappropriate expectations:
- Are my expectations realistic?
- Am I willing to persevere in spite of setbacks?

Control through power:
- Have I eliminated the use of anger as a tool?
- Am I willing to cooperate?

Specialness:
- Do I put myself in other people's shoes?
- Do I respect the opinions of others?

Tactics to Avoid Accountability

<u>Putting others on the defensive</u>:
- attacking their competency
- attacking them personally
- attacking the competency of those in authority (staff, managers, parents, etc.)
- claiming others don't appreciate any changes or efforts toward change that may have been made
- bringing up irrelevant issues
- letting others do all the work (use of silence)
- minimizing the situation
- demonstrating anger
- picking at details
- paying little or no attention

<u>Controlling information</u>:
- agreeing with no intention of following through
- saying whatever will please or satisfy at the moment (this includes saying "yes")

- leaving information out, distorting information, mentioning self-serving information only
- being intentionally vague
- confusing others by including too much detail or not enough
- refusing to give any information (silence)

<u>Controlling interactions</u>:

- listening selectively and hearing only what is self-serving
- diverting attention to minor points
- insisting s/he "forgot" (in order to avoid being held accountable)
- focusing on being "misunderstood" as opposed to addressing the issue
- shifting to blaming others and/or circumstances

Continuum of Behavior

RESPONSIBLE

HAS A PATTERN OF:

1. Obeying rules.
2. Keeping commitments; accepting responsibility.
3. Maintaining cooperative relationships.
4. Fulfilling obligations and working hard.
5. Considering others.
6. Being willing to listen; trusting others.
7. Working to earn the trust and the respect of others.
8. Dismissing irresponsible thoughts.

IRRESPONSIBLE/LEGAL

HAS A PATTERN OF:

1. Honoring commitments only when it is convenient or promises a payoff.
2. Lying because it's easy (more often by omission than by commission).
3. Letting others down.
4. Breaking rules.
5. Controlling others and events through manipulation, deceit, or intimidation.
6. Failing to persevere; quitting when something gets uncomfortable or hard.
7. Keeping secrets.
8. Finding irresponsible activity exciting.

IRRESPONSIBLE/ILLEGAL

HAS A PATTERN OF:

1. Breaking rules/the law.
2. Blaming others; criticizing others.
3. Exploiting others.
4. Engaging in frequent or continuous irresponsible thinking.
5. Thinking only of self.
6. Being unwilling to accept obligations; refusing to be held accountable.
7. Focusing on "not getting caught" and "beating the system"; getting away with something makes it okay.
8. Acting as if he/she is better than others; not seeing self as a criminal.
9. Living a secretive lifestyle; concealing lots of illegal activity.

THE NON-DICTIONARY OF ANOTHER USAGE

**—A Work in Progress—
(from draft #2, First Edition, 1998)**

THIS IS NOT A DICTIONARY! Although this collection of words, phrases (and, occasionally, motifs and other behaviors) is presented in dictionary form, we do not intend it to be understood or used as a dictionary in the standard sense. What we present are not stable usages and their equivalents. They are instead items of language that we have observed in practice whose meaning and intent regularly differ from what, in the pages that follow, we term "common usage." The items of "another usage" will usually sound the same as common usage, but intent and meaning will be different. Indeed, the overriding intent is "I don't want you to know what is really happening." It is a language use in which the speaker's goal is to avoid being held accountable.

The following list is appropriately used only when context has been fully taken into account. If you can establish a pattern of irresponsible behavior, you can be assured that it is accompanied by an underlying pattern of irresponsible thinking. That thinking will in turn be articulated by "another" language use, in which some of the following expressions, motifs, and behaviors, in the form we list or in other similar terms, will figure prominently. It is our hope that becoming familiar with the following words and phrases as representative of "another usage" will help you to "hear" what is being said in such circumstances. By means of the following "cues," you will find it possible to interpret better what is actually being said and simultaneously become better equipped to promote change.

Some cautions. Use of one or more of the following expressions is not itself sufficient to make someone an "irresponsible thinker"; for that purpose, the presence of an entire thought pattern must be established. Conversely, the simple attempt to prohibit the use of terms such as the following will not itself significantly curtail irresponsible thinking. When used appropriately, the following list can form a key component of effective interruption/change practices.

This non-dictionary is a work in progress. We are continuing the process of addition, correction, and refinement. We welcome your comments.

C.U. = Common Usage
I.U. = Irresponsible Usage
Exp. = Example

Basically

    C.U.   Fundamentally

    I.U.   "Basically" usually functions as a sign that something is about to be left out; lying by omission is about to be committed.

    Exp.   A new resident of the county jail comes to the counselor's office. As he begins to talk about himself he says "Basically this is my first incarceration." His record reveals that he has been in jail twice before. When pressed, he will likely produce a narrative about why the other incarcerations "don't count."

Boredom

- **C.U.** Lack of interest.
- **I.U.** Inability to engage in the excitement of irresponsible or criminal activity; inability to manipulate or use power over someone else.
- **Exp.** Mary is a girl who has been in trouble in school and has been caught smoking marijuana. She has been sent to summer camp for the first time. She is surrounded by activities: volleyball, swimming, crafts, hiking, etc. She complains of being bored: "There is nothing exciting to do."

"But I Feel"

- **C.U.** Used to express emotions and thoughts.
- **I.U.** Used to construct an excuse.
- **Exp.** Becky is furious at her parents for grounding her. When they point out that she has broken the ba-

sic rules about using the family car, she explodes, "But I was feeling upset with Gerry (her boy friend) and couldn't help it. It wasn't my fault."

Can't

- **C.U.** Unable to.
- **I.U.** Won't; unwilling to.
- **Exp.** Joshua has been asked to refrain from swearing in the class room. "I can't" he replies; "it's a habit."

Change

- **C.U.** To make different; to alter; to undergo variation or replacement (here, in the context of changing behavior patterns).
- **I.U.** The "change" is located only in the desired outcome, not in the behavior.
- **Exp.** Tammy has been eager to change her life. She is now sober and attending substance abuse groups. She comes in Monday morning feeling really down. "My old man is threatening to walk out on me" she says. "He says I'm no fun sober. I think I can drink a little with him on weekends and

still stay straight. I can't live without him." The group challenges Tammy, saying that this is not change. Tammy insists that it is.

Closeness

C.U. An intimate relationship; a relationship that feels comfortable.

I.U. A relationship that involves the other person being obedient and unquestioning.

Exp. The group is working on cooperative relationships. Danny says that he and his girl friend have a close relationship. "We are real close," he says. As the group continues it surfaces that Danny and his girlfriend are in a very one-sided relationship. He does the ordering, and she does the doing.

Crime

C.U. An act committed or omitted in violation of the law.

I.U. An act defined as "a crime" only when there is absolutely no other alternative available in the context. Otherwise, this is a word that is avoided.

Exp. The offender group was entirely made up of court referrals. To be a member of the group one had to have committed a crime. Ben, a new member, objected to the use of the word "criminal." "I haven't committed any crime," he insisted angrily. "What about the robbery?" the group members asked. "Oh that," Ben answered. "That wasn't a crime; I was high on crack."

Crisis (See *Emergency*)

Emergency

C.U. Occurrence or set of circumstances requiring immediate action.

I.U. Anything that is wanted at the time; what is felt to be important at the moment.

Exp. Sheila calls her fiancé, Freddie, at work. It is lunch time. Freddie works at Wendy's, and the restaurant is very busy. Sheila is told that Freddie can't come to the phone. She tells them it is an "emergency." When Freddie picks up the phone, she tells him to pick her up at 4 P.M. rather than 5 P.M. that afternoon.

Excitement

- **C.U.** Arousal of feelings.
- **I.U.** Rule or law breaking; doing harm.
- **Exp.** Janice cannot come down off the high. She has just stolen her first blouse from the shopping center. She is exhilarated from getting away with it. "Yeah, girl, it was exciting," she tells her friend.

Facts

- **C.U.** Deeds; acts; something that has actually happened.
- **I.U.** C.U. "facts" don't exist unless "I" say so and "I" define them. (Otherwise, C.U. "facts" are either ignored or openly dismissed.)
- **Exp.** Kelly is furious as she listens to her teacher and the teaching intern discuss her behavior in class. Kelly accepts none of what they have to say. "You're bogus," she screams. "The fact is neither of you ever liked me anyhow."

Failure

- **C.U.** The act or fact of being unsuccessful, falling short.
- **I.U.** Not being #1 or the "top dog"; not being an instant success; needing immediate returns.
- **Exp.** Harry, eleven hears old, is working with a social worker on his anger. He has agreed to practice taking a "time out." That afternoon Carl calls Harry a name. Harry and Carl get into a fight. The next day Harry complains to his social worker, "I tried it and it didn't work." (***Failure*** is variously expressed; see, e.g., *"I Tried It"*)

Fair

- **C.U.** To be just and honest, impartial; to work according to rules.
- **I.U.** To have an advantage; to get what one wants.
- **Exp.** "It's not fair anymore," complains Nathan. "I used to be able to tell her what to do. Now she's listening to those women at the shelter and getting ideas of her own."

Friend

- **C.U.** A person whom one knows well and is fond of.
- **I.U.** Someone who will do what I want when I want it; who will keep quiet about me; who agrees to break rules and commit crimes with me.
- **Exp.** In her spare time Jane works with adolescents as a volunteer. One of the young women, Cassandra, who is often in trouble, has asked Jane if she can borrow some lipstick. Jane has agreed. A few weeks later Cassandra asks Jane to take her across town to see an old boyfriend. Jane refuses. "Hey I thought you were my friend," Cassandra screams angrily, feeling betrayed. (Note: When Cassandra asks to borrow the lipstick, she is seeking to make that exchange the token of an "irresponsible friendship." Thus, when Jane agrees to the loan, Cassandra interprets that agreement as acknowledgment of such a relationship.)

Frustrated

- **C.U.** Not being able to fulfill desires or reach a desired objective.

I.U.	Finding no one else to blame; not being allowed to blame something outside of oneself.
Exp.	Janet glared furiously at her English teacher. Her frustration showed. Mr. Snow would except none of her reasons for a late paper. "I am tired of your excuses," he told Janet, "you have no one to blame but yourself."

Getting Involved

C.U.	Establishing a relationship; making commitments.
I.U.	Establishing a relationship based on sex only, a relationship of power not intimacy.
Exp.	Harold tells the psychologist he is "involved" with a woman named Shirley. Further sessions reveal that they see each other occasionally: Harold shows up and demands sex, and Shirley complies. Harold feels that she should be available to him when he wants.

Help

C.U.	To make things easier for a person; to assist; aid.

I.U.	From the irresponsible thinker's point of view: "You fix it for me"; "you do everything."
Exp.	Tony is sullen and withdrawn. He is back at Youth Detention for using drugs. He blames the local substance abuse center. "I asked for help and they put me on a waiting list. What did you expect me to do?"

Honesty

C.U.	Being truthful, trustworthy, and sincere.
I.U.	To tell intentions with no expectation of following through on them.
Exp.	Barbara, 8 years old, has been in trouble repeatedly over the past several years. She especially likes to hit her little sister Tamara. Her father has spoken to her, and Barbara has given a verbal agreement to stop this behavior. Her father hears Tamara crying and goes to investigate. Barbara defiantly yells at her dad, "I didn't mean to."

"I Did Everything I Could"

- **C.U.** I did everything I could think of; I tried all resources.
- **I.U.** I did what I could until it got too hard or became inconvenient.
- **Exp.** Luanda has promised her friends that she will meet them at 4 P.M. at the pizza parlor. She never shows up. The next day she explains to one of those friends that she was watching a movie and then her boyfriend called. "What's the big deal," she asks, "I did everything I could."

"I Didn't Mean To" (See *Honesty*)

"I'll Do My Best" (See *"I'll Try"*)

"I'll Try"

- **C.U.** I will make the best effort I possibly can.
- **I.U.** I will make an effort until it gets unpleasant, uncomfortable, or hard.
- **Exp.** Laurie has been in and out of the Youth Detention Center several times for shoplifting. She is

talking with her probation officer. He is setting out some expectations for staying out of trouble. "I'll try," replies Laurie. Two days later Laurie is picked up again by the police on additional shoplifting charges. She reports that her friends dared her to steal a blouse from Walmart and she gave in. (Cf. *"I Did Everything I Could"*)

"I'm Listening"

    C.U.   I am attending closely; I am taking advice.

    I.U.   I am waiting for someone to say something I want to hear.

    Exp.   María sits bored and silent as her mother tells her what it was like not knowing where María was all night. Her mother accuses her of not listening. María replies, "I <u>am</u> listening." Finally feeling tired and frustrated the mother tells María to go to her room. María perks up and is gone in a flash.

Impatience

    C.U.   Annoyance because of delay.

I.U.   Intimidation; demonstration of anger (an implied threat).

Exp.   As Loretta explains why they are out of money, Pat begins to tap his fingers on the table. She begins to feel frightened and rushes through her explanation. She finds herself making things up hoping to please him.

Independent

C.U.   Self-confident; self-reliant; free to accept or reject the influence and control of others.

I.U.   Not willing to be accountable to anybody.

Exp.   "No way," replies Michael, "I like being independent." Janet has asked Michael for a commitment in helping to raise their son. Michael shows up now and then, but there is never anything Janet can count on.

Injustice

C.U.   Unfairness.

I.U.   Getting caught, not getting away with breaking rules or breaking the law.

Exp.	Gerry tries to sneak out of the house after his parents have fallen asleep. This is against the household rules. His dad gets up for a glass of water, hears some noise, and investigates. He finds Gerry slipping out the window. Gerry's dad takes away car privileges for the next month. Gerry had been told ahead of time about the expectation and the consequences. "This isn't fair," Gerry complains.

Intention

C.U.	Mental attitude at the time of doing an act; aim or purpose.
I.U.	An attitude, real or merely claimed, that when disclosed should absolve one of all responsibility.
Exp.	Ramón gets arrested for reckless driving and for driving while intoxicated. He is angry and upset and feels this isn't fair. He explains to the arresting officer that he didn't intend to get drunk, drive, and run a light. He had intended to have a few drinks and go home. (Cf. *Honesty*)

"I Tried It" (See *Failure*)

"I Trust You"
- C.U. I believe in your honesty and reliability; I have confidence in you.
- I.U. You will do me favors and keep my secrets; you will give me what I want.
- Exp. Tanisha is assigned a new counselor. She is upset and unhappy about the change. Tanisha has been expelled from high school for a variety of offenses. She had been working with her old counselor for 6 months at the local mental health center. Tanisha liked her old counselor. She and Tanisha spent most of the time talking about how unfair the school had been to her. Tanisha isn't at all sure she can trust a new counselor as she did the old one.

It's Hard
- C.U. This will require effort; this will be difficult.
- I.U. I am not willing to put in the effort or to make the commitment.

Exp. John has been talking to the group for several weeks about wanting to change. He expresses how much he never wants to return to jail again. He agonizes over how his past choices have hurt his family. When the group presses him about making changes in his daily life, like going to work on a regular basis, he replies, "It's hard." Time and again the group presses him for commitments and over and over again he answers every suggestion with "But it's hard."

Justice

C.U. Fairness; upholding of the law.
I.U. Getting what I want; not getting caught.
Exp. Sol has been caught smoking marijuana in the school bathroom. The overworked principal decides to give Sol a break and let the incident go. That afternoon Sol crows to his friends, "the system really works." It seems just to him. (Cf. *Fair*)

Lonely

C.U. Alone; solitary; longing for friends.

I.U.	Absent anyone to control or manipulate.
Exp.	Tyrone has been in jail for a week and reports to a correctional officer that he is "lonely." He states that he misses his "woman." Later, the officer grants him a phone call. He watches as Tyrone becomes animated while giving his "woman" a series of orders over the phone. After he hangs up Tyrone feels much better.

Manhood

C.U.	Possession of manly qualities.
I.U.	"I can outwit others and get what I want, get my way."
Exp.	Michael cannot believe his case worker is encouraging him to walk away from certain situations, like the one in which he was called a "snitch." "I can talk my way around that S.O.B. any day," Michael said, clearly proud of himself. "He always ends up eating his words. He does what I say."

Objectively

    C.U.   Having existence independent of the mind; real.

    I.U.   From my point of view.

    Exp.   "I <u>am</u> looking at it objectively!" Carl hollers, "I'm telling you the way I see it."

Perfect

    C.U.   Flawless; having the property of excellence.

    I.U.   Pertaining to a situation in which I get everything I want.

    Exp.   Jerome's mom sits on the other side of the visitation window. Tears are streaming down her cheeks. "Perfect," says Jerome. "I should be out by this afternoon." His mom has just told him that she has mortgaged her home in order to bail him out.

Personality Conflict

    C.U.   A situation in which people are not able to get along, not able to work together.

    I.U.   To be unable to control another person; one person won't do what the other says to do.

Exp.	There is obvious tension in the teen support group as the facilitator comes into the room. She asks what's going on. Group members look at each other. Finally one speaks up and states that there is a personality conflict in the group. Danny says: "It's a personality conflict. Either George goes, or I do." The group discusses the situation for a while. What becomes clear is that Danny is used to "calling the shots" and being in charge. George is used to the same role. Neither can control the other.

Police

C.U.	Governmental department for keeping order.
I.U.	Anyone holding me accountable or checking up on me.
Exp.	Marjorie looks at her sister with hate in her eyes. "What are you, the police?" she asks. Her sister has just reminded her of her promise not to smoke in the house. Their parents are not home.

Police State

- **C.U.** An authoritarian social unit controlled in a military-like manner.
- **I.U.** Existence of rules.
- **Exp.** A mother, frustrated with the lack of consistency at home, has put up a set of rules on the refrigerator. They include expectations for chores around the house and consequences for not doing them. Her teenaged daughter objects angrily, "Hey, what is this, a police state?"

Power

- **C.U.** Ability to influence; possessing great force or authority.
- **I.U.** Control over others (i.e., you only have power to abuse it).
- **Exp.** Larissa is given the position of group leader. She proceeds to belittle Jamie and Ellen and make fun of their discomfort. When questioned about this she replies, "I'm group leader, aren't I?"

Powerless

    C.U.   Weak; impotent.

    I.U.   Unable to control others.

    Exp.   Lee is in in-patient substance abuse treatment. He has been restless and uncooperative in the last several groups. When confronted he gets angry. "I feel powerless," he shouts. As the group continues to discuss what Lee means, it becomes clear that he is angry because others aren't doing what he wants them to do.

Pride

    C.U.   Sense of one's own dignity; self-respect; an overly high opinion of oneself.

    I.U.   Sense of being better than others.

    Exp.   Joshua is satisfied. He watches David walk away. Joshua has got the better of him. Joshua feels proud and content. "I'm better than David anyway, and David might as well get used to it."

Reasonable (See also *Unreasonable*)

    C.U.   Sound judgement; sensible; not extreme.

I.U.	Whatever I agree with; anything that goes along with what I want.
Exp.	Terry hadn't expected his parents to be so reasonable. In spite of the fact that he had broken curfew for the third time in a row, they agreed to let him use the car again tomorrow night.

Relax

C.U.	To rest; to become less intense.
I.U.	To know no one is watching me; know no one is able to hold me accountable.
Exp.	Ricky is complaining to the correctional officer. New rules are requiring the officers to keep closer watch on the inmates. In addition, frequent cell checks are being made. "I can't relax," he complains.

Resentment

C.U.	A sense of being offended.
I.U.	A sense of being unjustly treated by people because they aren't willing to tolerate excuse-making and/or irresponsible behavior.

Exp.	Tim's mom and girl friend have always listened to his irresponsible excuse-making. Lately, they have been unwilling to put up with him. Tim tells his counselor "I'm feeling resentful that they're not giving me the support I need. That's what they should be doing!" The counselor rephrases: "You mean you're disappointed?" Tim: "Yeah, my girl friend even said she didn't want to hear my 'bullshit' any more."

Respect

C.U.	High regard.
I.U.	Fear.
Exp.	Sam cuts in line in front of Ken. Ken angrily challenges him: "Let's see some respect." Sam backs off. Ken has a reputation for dealing harshly with those who "get in his way."

Responsible

C.U.	Answerable for obligations and duties; accountable for behavior.

I.U.	Willing to admit to being wrong only when there is nothing else to do; taking care of "me" only.
Exp.	Silas is angry at the group. They are accusing him of being irresponsible. This is the fourth time in jail. Silas has a wife and three children. "I do the time, don't I," he angrily counters back to them. "I own up to what I do."

Right

C.U.	In accordance with justice, law, or morality; in accordance with fact.
I.U.	What I want at the time.
Exp.	Pam insists, "It was the right thing to do. I did it to protect him. If he had known I was using again, it would have broken his heart." (She wants to continue using and doesn't want him to know.) (Cf. *Fair*)

Satisfy

C.U.	To fulfill requirements; to comply with obligations or rules; to accept an outcome (passive).
I.U.	To get my way; to get what I want.

Exp. Sonya is called to the principal's office. She has been in trouble most of the year and has been told she might not pass eighth grade. She receives the news that she will move on to the ninth grade with a sense of satisfaction. She has managed again to get what she wants: "Hey, man, I'm satisfied."

Self-Esteem

C.U. Belief in oneself; self-respect.

I.U. "I get what I want"; "I please myself."

Exp. Monica is a member of a group of repeat offenders. "I steal because I have low self-esteem," she tells the group. Another group member asks her, "Where was your low self-esteem when you snatched that poor lady's purse?"

Support

C.U. To help; to comfort; to provide assistance.

I.U. To do what I want; to do what I tell you to do.

Exp. "All I'm asking for is a little support," Emily says. Her boyfriend has turned down her request to drive her over to her girlfriends' house. These girlfriends are drug users, and Emily has sworn to give up using drugs.

"Take Advantage Of"

C.U. Get the most out of; benefit from; learn what you can.

I.U. Rip off; manipulate; get off easy.

Exp. Ralph is angry during group. He is in a program to deal with substance abuse. He feels he is working hard. He seems resentful. After some prodding, he states: "I can't work this program. Too many people come into it just trying to 'beat their case.' They take advantage." (Note: Ralph too is "taking advantage": by complaining about others who are "taking advantage.")

Taking Care Of Business

C.U. Fulfilling obligations.

I.U. Getting done what is important to me; not seeing it as anyone else's concern—whatever it is; others are not supposed to ask questions.

Exp. A counselor sees Sam in Dan's room after lights out. "What's up?" he asks the boys, "you should be in your own rooms." "Nothing," Sam replies, "just taking care of business."

Trust

C.U. A firm belief in the honesty and reliability of another; acting on that belief.

I.U. A firm belief that an individual will do what you want, including keeping your secrets, breaking rules, and committing crimes with you.

Exp. Tabatha and Nancy were no longer on speaking terms with each other. Nancy had thought she could trust Tabatha. They had been good friends ever since entering the treatment program. Last Saturday Nancy's boyfriend successfully smuggled her some dope. Nancy confided in Tabatha, and Tabatha told one of the counselors. "I thought I could trust you," screamed Nancy.

Truth

C.U. In agreement with reality or facts.

I.U.	Relating just enough to satisfy.
Exp.	Bobby's wife sits across from him dejectedly. "I've told you the truth," he repeats. He has admitted to taking a little marijuana and having a cup of coffee with her girl friend. He thinks that amount of information will satisfy Patty, and she will stop questioning him. (Patty knows that he was out with her girl friend last night and stayed the night. She also knows that he used drugs after promising not to.

"Truth Will Out"

C.U.	Justice will be served; the guilty will be punished.
I.U.	I focus only on what I want others to see; whatever (else) I have done wrong will go unnoticed.
Exp.	A resident of the county jail is talking to a counselor. He has a long criminal history of deceitful practices. He is intensely focused on his declaration of innocence in the latest offense. "The truth will out" he continues to repeat (meaning I <u>am</u> going to get away with what I have just done).

Unfair (See *Injustice*)

Unreasonable (See also *Reasonable*)
- C.U. Showing little sense; excessive.
- I.U. Anything I don't want.
- Exp. "I can't understand how you can be so unreasonable," Brent complained. "I'm just asking for a small favor." Brent had run away several times from the group home. He was now asking to be allowed to visit a friend over the weekend. The house counselor has refused the request.

Wrong
- C.U. Unlawful; improper; incorrect.
- I.U. Too risky or too dangerous.
- Exp. Reiko is talking with her friends about being caught breaking curfew. "It was dumb," she says. "It was the wrong thing to do; my parents had been watching me too closely."

"You Don't Understand"
- C.U. You are not comprehending the meaning.

I.U. You aren't giving me what I want.

Exp. Nancy is explaining to her teacher why her paper is late for the third day in a row. After listening to several minutes of excuses he has heard many times before, he tells Marcy that the paper will be marked late and receive a lower grade. "But you don't understand, "Marcy glares at the teacher; "I have explained it to you."

"You're Right, I Was Wrong"

C.U. Admission of a mistake.

I.U. Not principally an admission of error; instead a statement setting up an expectation that now something will be given in return.

Exp. "O.K., O.K.," says Alice to the police officer. "You're right and I'm wrong." When the officer proceeds to arrest her she feels betrayed. She thought they had a deal. After all, she humiliated herself by the "false" admission and now she hasn't received anything in return.

Sousa, Peacock, Sousa

The firm of Sousa, Peacock, Sousa & Associates is located in Champaign, Illinois. It provides individual and group counseling as well as parent education and partner abuse groups. The firm also conducts trainings, educational seminars, and systems analyses and designs and implements programs for social-service agencies, schools, and businesses based on a cognitive restructuring approach to human behavior.

The firm members encompass a wide variety of backgrounds and possess a number of different skills that enable the company to respond flexibly and capably to the different needs and specific requirements of a broad spectrum of clients.

Capabilities encompassed:
- Licensure and certification in the fields of psychological counseling (both individual and group work), education, criminal justice, addiction, and mediation.
- Skills and application capabilities covering children adults, and both men and women; fluency in Spanish.
- Backgrounds in public speaking, media appearances, workshops and seminars, and published writing; multi-cultural.
- All founding partners are certified Corrective Thinking Trainers (by Koerner and Fawcett) and have extensive experience in the field; we are thus able to offer certification trainings.

Sousa, Peacock, Sousa & Associates has collective work experience in a wide variety of settings including schools, social service agencies, mental health agencies, alternative educational settings, group homes for children, and corrections.

Not only have firm members designed and implemented programs in schools, correctional systems, and in social service and mental health agencies but we have experience as well in redesigning ongoing programs and in helping to enhance the professional expertise and effectiveness of existing staff.

Corrective Thinking materials are available upon request.